INSPIRATIONAL

BASEBALL STORIES

FOR YOUNG READERS

*21 Incredible True Narratives to Inspire
and Educate Young Baseball Lovers About
the Values of Life*

JOHN J. LEWIS

CONTENT INDEX

Introduction *7*

Chapter 1: SHOTS OF MAGIC
The Soul And Lessons Of Baseball 11

Chapter 2: MIKE PIAZZA
The Transition From Shadow to Light ..15

Chapter 3: ROBERTO CLEMENTE
Commitment Beyond the Diamond....... 25

Chapter 4: BABE RUTH
The Giant of American Baseball.............31

Chapter 5: JIM ABBOTT
Master of Self-Esteem on The Diamond.. 37

Chapter 6: LOU GEHRIG
Real Luck in Life..................................... 41

Chapter 7: KIRK GIBSON
The King of Impossible Homeruns........ 47

Chapter 8: JOE DI MAGGIO
Hero of 56 Jokes..................................... 53

Chapter 9: MO'NE DAVIS
Baseball is also Women's 59

Chapter 10: JACKIE ROBINSON
Beyond the Diamond for True Equality ...63

Chapter 11: MARIANO RIVERA
When the Dream Becomes Legend 69

Chapter 12: DEREK JETER
The Diamond Wizard 75

Chapter 13: YOGI BERRA
The Man Who Spoke With Smiles 81

Chapter 14: DARRYL STRAWBERRY
From Storm to Rebirth 89

Chapter 15: KEN GRIFFEY JR
The Baseball Smile 95

Chapter 16: SATCHEL PAIGE
Defiance of Injustice 101

Chapter 17: HAMMERIN' HANK
From Challenge to Legend 107

Chapter 18: TOMMY JOHN
The Art of Rebirth..............................113

Chapter 19: TY COBB
Baseball's Indomitable Flame 119

Chapter 20: WILLIE MAYS
Indominability...................................125

Chapter 21: WALTER JOHNSON
The Silent Speed of the Great Train...131

Chapter 22: CHRISTY MATHEWSON
Baseball's Historic Turning Point 137

Conclusion 143

Bibliography...147

INTRODUCTION

S ink into pure emotion.
You find yourself in a packed stadium, enveloped by the growing buzz of thousands of voices, with every heartbeat synchronizing with the exclamations around you.

The atmosphere is imbued with the sweet aroma of caramel and cotton candy.

A pleasant aroma of hot dogs and freshly toasted buns wafts in from afar, awakening memories of days spent sharing laughter and hopes in the stands.

Then, like thunder in the distance, thunderous applause erupts.

A formidable batter has just sent the ball across the field, thanks to a majestic pitch! This, my friend, is the palpable beating heart of baseball: an overwhelming mix of sensations, moments which make you hold your breath, and an uninterrupted flow of emotions catapults you to every corner of the field.

Baseball is not just about impressive physical gestures and pure adrenaline.

Behind every action on the field are deep tactics, a mélange of skill and foresight, and a continuous dance between strength and strategy. It is a stage on which the everyday is elevated to the status of the extraordinary, where all, regardless of their history, can rise as unexpected heroes and where the most profound desires take shape.

In the coming chapters, I will guide you on an adventure along the intricate paths of the sport, traversing that hallowed green rectangle, the stage of countless dramas and triumphs, revealing the stories and legends which have helped shape baseball.

We are not simply recounting sporting adventures.

These pages are about immeasurable determination, teamwork, and the unstoppable capacity of the human spirit to overcome any obstacle. Stories which show how, in life, as in baseball, every single step and choice can trigger a fantastic chain of events, creating memorable wonders.

Each page you flip through invites you to dive in, reflect, and be inspired.

Whether you find yourself hitting a ball in the middle of a stadium or navigating the complexities of everyday life, every action, every risk, and every moment of courage has the power to transform into a transcendental experience.

And you, like any great athlete, possess the potential to make every moment of your life truly special.

Baseball, for many people, is not just a sport: it is an odyssey, a reenactment of the challenges, struggles, and triumphs we face throughout our lives. Every detail of the game, from the plot of a single inning to the overall dynamic of a season, can be seen as a parallel of the moments which define us as individuals.

When a batter steps to the plate, eyes fixed on the pitcher, it's is as if he is faced with life's big decisions. In that brief instant, everything stops. The choices made in that critical moment - wait or hit, advance or stay - are reminiscent of the existential crossroads we all face.

The bat, heavy in the batter's hands, is like the weight of responsibility each of us carries. Each pitch is a new beginning and challenge, and our approach determines our path.

The pitch itself, with its clearly defined bases and lines, can be compared to the path of life. There are rules, goals to reach, and obstacles to overcome.

The bases represent the milestones of existence: youth, maturity, old age, and, finally, the return home at the culmination of our existence.

Teams, meanwhile, are more than just groups of players.

They are like the communities, families, or groups of friends which support us throughout our lives. Each player, with his specific role, be he pitcher, catcher, outfielder, or infielder, represents the people we meet along the way, each influencing our lives in unique and unpredictable ways.

And then there are the unforgettable moments.

The home runs that float through the air like those rare and precious moments of pure exhilaration in life, the fast pitches which surprise and challenge us. These acrobatic defensive plays remind us we can overcome even the most significant obstacles with skill and determination.

However baseball, like life, is not just about moments of triumph.

There are also defeats, mistakes, and moments of doubt.

And just like in life, it is the ability to pick yourself up after a fall, to learn from your mistakes, and to keep pushing forward with hope and determination which truly defines a player - and a person. It is not just a game; it is a journey.

Like any journey, it teaches, challenges, and ultimately reveals who we are. Through its games, seasons, legends, and protagonists, we are offered a unique perspective on the flow of life and the intrinsic beauty of every moment we experience.

Once you have finished reading this book, I kindly invite you to leave a review on Amazon.
I have worked hard on this product and would love to get your opinion.
https://www.amazon.com/review/create-review?asin=B0CLNH378L

Now dive into the heart of the diamond and some of its most outstanding protagonists of all time!

Chapter 1

SHOTS OF MAGIC
THE SOUL AND LESSONS OF BASEBALL

Baseball stands as a beacon in an era dominated by technology and frenzy, not just as a sport but as a reminder of fundamental values and more straightforward and genuine moments. This book is not just about baseball. It is a deep exploration of the souls and lives the game has touched and transformed.

With each page, immerse yourself in the intricate plots of stories which resonate with pure emotion. From the up-and-coming hitter who faces the unimaginable pressure of loaded bases, to the pitcher who, after a losing streak, discovers the strength to pick up the ball and pitch with renewed passion. Each tale becomes a microcosm of life itself, reflecting the challenges we all face, the lessons we learn, and the victories, big or small, which celebrate our indomitable spirit.

For you, young friend, holding this book in your hands, there is a clear message: life, like baseball, is a game of patience, resilience, determination, and passion. Through the challenges and setbacks, there is always an opportunity for a comeback, a chance for a home run. And as each story unfolds, a profound moral truth emerges, a universal lesson which goes beyond the field, reaching the heart.

It is not just an invitation to play but a call to live with intensity, to understand there is a story, a soul, and a lesson behind every pitch, hit, and decision. This work is meant to be a journey into the essence of baseball and, by extension, into the heart of the human experience.

It is a hymn to humanity, the struggle, the love of the game, and self-discovery through challenges. For this reason, the book analyzes the exploits of 21 of the most famous players ever. These characters, in turn, recall 21 characteristics which are fundamental to your success in life.

They are:

Humility
Compassion
Authenticity
Self-esteem
Gratitude
Determination
Being oneself
Fighting prejudices
Equality
The impossible becomes possible
From dream to reality
The art of smiling

Reinventing
Relationship between generations
Justice
Courage
Rebirth
Tenacity
Indominability
Speed
Innovation

We often traverse a maze of choices, experiences, and emotions at the beginning of life. In our race to define who we are and our place in the world, there is an inner compass of essential virtues which can guide us toward a meaningful life.

Imagine you have a mosaic in front of you. Each title represents a virtue: humility, compassion, authenticity, and so on. These titles are beautiful and luminous, but we can see only the whole picture when we put them together. This mosaic represents the complexity and beauty of our existence.

Being very young, you can start building this mosaic knowing each virtue has a unique role. Speed and determination can drive you to pursue your dreams. At the same time, the art of smiling and self-confidence will give you the strength to face challenges with joy and confidence. But it is not only about pursuing your goals. Fighting prejudices and cultivating equality and justice allows us to create a world where everyone can prosper.

Reinventing oneself and finding the courage to change and grow emphasizes the importance of rebirth and adaptation in a constantly changing world.

It is essential to remain authentic, to be true to oneself and others, and to cultivate one's individuality while maintaining a connection with past and future generations.

These virtues are abstract concepts and tools which, when cultivated, can guide us through life with grace, determination, and love.

And like any mosaic, each title we add becomes more straightforward and more beautiful.

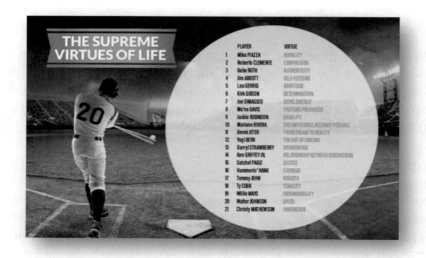

Chapter 2

MIKE PIAZZA
THE TRANSITION FROM SHADOW TO LIGHT

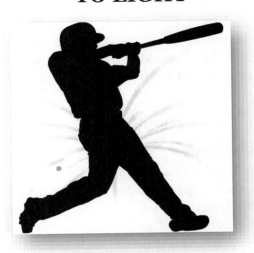

Baseball has always had a special place at the heart of American sports.
It has given birth to heroes and legends, and one of these is Mike Piazza, a player whose story resonates with passion, determination, and an indomitable will to overcome any obstacle.

Imagine being in New York, inside one of the most iconic stadiums in the world.
Over 50,000 people around you, each waiting for a magical moment.
The tension is palpable. You can feel the crowd holding its breath as a man approaches the platform. That man is Mike Piazza.
Mike did not have the advantages of his peers.

He was not considered a prodigy, nor was he destined for greatness in his high school days. However he possessed an unstoppable determination and a burning passion for baseball. This love for the game took him through the minor leagues, where his skill and dedication opened the door to the major ones.

In his career, Mike has done it all.

He hit decisive home runs, led teams to the playoffs, and set records. However more than any accomplishment or performance, Mike Piazza symbolized what is possible when you combine talent, hard work, and unparalleled dedication.

Yet who was Mike really off the court?

A man characterized by the same humility and determination he showed on the court.

Despite his extraordinary success, he always remembered where he came from and who he was. His story is not just one of a great baseball player, on the contrary it's of an individual who, through adversity, demonstrated how one can overcome any obstacle with the right mindset and dedication.

This is why, dear friend, don't just think of a baseball player when you hear the name Mike Piazza. Think of a symbol of hope, determination, and reckoning. Let his story inspire you and show you how to reach for the stars with the right mindset and commitment.

All great stories start somewhere.

Mike's story begins in a small town in Pennsylvania.

He was born into a family of modest beginnings. His childhood had no glamour or promise of a stellar baseball career. However he had a dream fuelled by hours spent watching games on television and imagining himself in the middle of those green fields.

When he was selected in the 62nd round of the MLB draft, many may have thought it was the end of his run. Yet for

Mike, it was only the beginning. In every workout and game in the minor leagues, he displayed a grit and passion which few possessed.

To be picked so late and then become a star is a proof of his dedication, hard work, and talent.

Outstanding Performance: Piazza set the record for the most home runs hit by a catcher in MLB history, a testament to his remarkable batting ability. He had a career batting average of 308 and hit 427 home runs in total.

He was not the most talented or the most physically gifted. Still, he had something which could not be measured: an immense heart, an unusual determination, and an uncommon humility. In a world where many young athletes try to get noticed, Mike remained silent, letting his performances speak for him.

He loved actions, not words. This humility protected him from many traps which have consumed other promising athletes. He resisted the temptation to fall into excesses and distractions, always focusing on his main goal: to become one of the best.

And then there was his determination. Every time he was rejected and told he wasn't good enough, Mike used those words as fuel.

He never allowed himself to give up, no matter how hard the road was. And in this determination, he found the strength to keep going, overcome every obstacle, and prove all his detractors wrong.

And, in the end, all his hard work paid off.

His MLB career was nothing less than spectacular, and his rise to success showed it is possible to reach unimaginable heights with the right combination of talent, determination, and dedication.

More than his performance on the field, the legacy of Mike Piazza continues to inspire.

Mike Piazza has had numerous memorable moments in his career. Still, one of the most emotional and evocative occurred on September 21, 2001. This event is mainly well known not only for its sporting implications but also for its historical and cultural context.

After the terrorist attacks of September 11, 2001, the United States was immersed in a state of grief, shock, and mourning. New York City, in particular, was at the center of this tragedy, having suffered the destruction of the World Trade Center Twin Towers.

Baseball, like many other activities, had been suspended immediately after the attacks.

When Major League Baseball resumed games, the first major sporting event in New York after September 11 was between the New York Mets and the Atlanta Braves at Shea Stadium on September 21st.

The atmosphere was tense. Many wondered whether holding significant public events so soon after such a devastating attack was appropriate or safe. The audience was full of emotion, with a mixture of grief for the loss and determination to show the resilience of New York and the United States.

Against this backdrop, Mike Piazza stepped up to bat with the Mets trailing by a run in the eighth inning. And he did something extraordinary: he hit a two-run homer, putting the Mets ahead. Shea Stadium erupted in a frenzy of joy. This was not just an ordinary home run in a typical baseball game. It symbolized resilience, determination, and hope for a grieving city and nation.

For many, that home run became a cathartic moment, a brief respite from grief, and a celebration of New York City's ability to endure and thrive in adversity. And for that, Mike Piazza's home run on September 21st, 2001, is remembered as one of the most emotional and significant moments in American sports history.

In addition to this historic moment, Mike Piazza had many other occasions where he electrified the fans.

- **Debut with the Mets**. In his first year with the New York Mets in 1998, after being acquired from the Florida Marlins, Piazza immediately made his presence felt. Fans were thrilled by the acquisition, and he responded by batting .348 with 23 home runs in 109 games that season.

- **2000 World Series**. Although the Mets failed to win the 2000 World Series against the New York Yankees, Piazza had highlights, including some home runs, which kept Mets fans on the edge.

- **Duel with Roger Clemens**. During the 2000 World Series, Piazza had a famous clash with Yankees pitcher Roger Clemens. After Clemens threw close to his head during the regular season, the tension between the two was palpable, culminating in an incident in which Clemens threw the fragment of a broken bat in Piazza's direction. This incident increased the drama and intensity of the series.

- **Outfield against the Braves in 1999**. During the 1999 pennant race, Piazza hit a grand slam against the rival Atlanta Braves, further cementing his hero status among Mets fans.

- **Hall of Fame induction**. In 2016, Mike Piazza was inducted into the Baseball Hall of Fame, recognizing his incredible talent and contribution to the game. During the ceremony, fans cheered him on for his astonishing career.

- **Decisive home runs**. During his career with the Mets and other teams, Piazza hit multiple decisive home runs which overturned the outcome of games, sending fans into a frenzy.

- **Catcher's home run record**. Mike Piazza holds the MLB record for the most home runs a catcher hits. This accomplishment demonstrates his extraordinary offensive skills in the position.

- **Last appearance as a Met**. In his last game with the Mets in 2005, Piazza received a standing ovation from the fans at Shea Stadium, an emotional moment highlighting his incredible team career.

Thanks to his ability to play under pressure and respond at critical moments, Piazza gave the fans countless memories. His every appearance at the plate was a potential electrifying moment, and he rarely disappointed.

His story teaches us it does not matter where we come from, what obstacles we face, or how many times we fail; how we react to these challenges matters. We can overcome anything with humility, determination, and commitment and achieve our wildest dreams.

The story of Mike Piazza is not just a baseball story.

It is a story of life.

It is a reminder no matter how impossible the odds may seem, anything is possible with the right mindset and commitment. And in this message, there is a lesson for us all.

Determination and humility are two qualities which, although seemingly different, can coexist harmoniously and synergistically within an individual. Exploring the relationship between these two virtues can offer a deep understanding of how they can work together to bring personal and professional success.

Determination is a firm decision to achieve a goal or overcome an obstacle. It is a driving force which motivates an individual to persist, regardless of challenges or adversity. It is an inner spark which says: "*I will never give up!*".

Humility is the ability to recognize one's limitations and imperfections. It is not submission or lack of self-esteem but rather an authentic awareness of oneself and one's place in the world.

Humility enables an individual to remain open to learning and change.

The phrase *"I know that I do not know"*, is attributed to Socrates and is a fundamental pillar of Socratic philosophy. This expression is often cited as the *"Socratic irony"*, but it has a deeper meaning and several implications.

First of all, the phrase suggests an acknowledgment of ignorance. Socrates believed true wisdom comes not from claiming to know everything rather from seeking and acknowledging what one does not know.

The admission of ignorance is the first step in seeking truth and knowledge. If a person thinks he knows everything, he will have no reason to ask questions or seek further information.

The statement also reflects humility. At a time when many philosophers proclaimed they had answers to big questions, Socrates distinguished himself by admitting the limits of his knowledge.

Socrates' statement can also be seen as a criticism of the complacency of Athenian society at the time. Many citizens were convinced of the superiority of their culture and knowledge. Socrates challenged this presumption.

In summary, *"I know that I do not know"* is a powerful statement emphasizing the importance of intellectual humility, recognition of the limits of one's knowledge, and the relentless pursuit of truth.

Determination drives a person to give their all, to keep striving, and not to settle. Humility, on the other hand, ensures this struggle does not become blind ambition or arrogance. Humility can modulate determination, guaranteeing a person remains open to criticism and ready to learn from mistakes.

While determination can lead to success, humility allows a person to manage success in a balanced way, recognizing the contribution of others and maintaining a realistic perspective.

Imagine climbing a mountain. Determination drives you up, even when your muscles ache and the summit seems unreachable. However humility allows you to ask for help when you need it, listen to the advice of those who have climbed the mountain before you, and recognize when it is time to stop and rest.

In career and life, people who have both determination and humility often achieve success more sustainably. These are the people who not only achieve their goals, they do so in a way which respects others and recognizes the value of the journey and the destination.

Too much of one quality without the other can lead to problems. Too much determination without humility can result in arrogance or insensitivity.

Too much humility without resolution can lead to passivity or lack of ambition.
So, while both of these qualities are valuable, their balance and interaction can create a powerful formula for personal and professional success.

In addition to his achievements on the field, Piazza has also been an ambassador for the game. He has represented baseball worldwide, helping to spread the sport's popularity. He has also used his platform for charity, contributing to numerous causes and helping those less fortunate.

Piazza retired in 2008, however his impact on the game will continue forever.

HUMILITY

Is recognizing one's limitations and imperfections, appreciating others for their contributions, and setting ego aside in favor of the greater good.

Humility is fundamental to a life of value. It provides a solid foundation for personal growth, improved relationships, and a deeper, more authentic understanding of the world around us.

Chapter 3

ROBERTO CLEMENTE
COMMITMENT BEYOND THE DIAMOND

In the warm summer evenings in Puerto Rico, a young boy dreamed of making a difference in baseball and the world. This boy was Roberto Clemente. Every time he stepped onto the field, he was a vision: elegance in movement, precision in play, and a heart which beats for justice.

Roberto was not only an outstanding athlete, he was a man of deep conviction.

He spent his career fighting against prejudice, challenging injustice, and using his platform as a baseball player to help others. His talent was undeniable, with over 3,000 hits in his career and numerous awards. However his true greatness lays beyond the numbers.

Clemente was driven by a deep sense of duty to his community. After each season, he would return to Puerto Rico and dedicate himself to humanitarian work. During his career, he helped countless young people, providing them with education, training, and hope.

Yet the true measure of a man is seen in his actions. Roberto Clemente proved his worth as a player and human being when he lost his life in a tragic plane crash while bringing humanitarian aid to Nicaragua after a devastating earthquake.

Roberto Clemente represents much more than baseball talent to you, young fan. He represents compassion, commitment, and integrity. He is a shining example of how to use your position and skill to make a difference. Let Clemente's story inspire you to pursue your dreams with determination, to fight for what you believe in, and to use every opportunity to make a positive mark on the world.

Roberto Enrique Clemente Walker was born on August 18, 1934, in Carolina, Puerto Rico, when the island faced economic and social challenges. He lived in poverty, where many families constantly struggled to search for opportunities and resources.

Carolina, although a city close to the capital, San Juan, had rural areas, and many families were involved in farming to make ends meet. Clemente's family were agricultural workers, and Roberto worked in the sugar fields with his family from a young age. This type of work is physically demanding and requires many hours in the sun.

In addition to economic challenges, Clemente faced cultural and racial difficulties when he started playing baseball professionally in the United States. Latino athletes, like Clemente, often faced prejudice and discrimination in Major League Baseball during the 1950s and 1960s.

Despite his extraordinary abilities on the field, Clemente was not exempt from such obstacles.

This background helped shape Clemente's character and determination to overcome adversity and give his best.

Tragically, Clemente died in a plane crash on December 31st, 1972, while attempting to deliver aid to earthquake victims in Nicaragua. The plane, overloaded with supplies, crashed shortly after takeoff from San Juan, Puerto Rico. He was 38 years old.

Clemente began his Major League Baseball career with the Pittsburgh Pirates in 1955. He played with the Pirates for his entire career, which lasted 18 seasons until 1972.

Roberto Clemente was an outstanding player and had many memorable moments during his baseball career.

- **MLB debut**. Clemente made his major league debut on April 17, 1955, against the Brooklyn Dodgers. From this moment, many fans and insiders sensed they were witnessing the rise of an exceptional talent.

- **1960 World Series**. Although his performance in the 1971 World Series is more celebrated, Clemente also played a vital role for the Pirates in their 1960 World Series victory over the New York Yankees. He had a .310 batting average in that series.

- **Four batting titles**. During his career, Clemente won four batting titles in the National League, demonstrating his consistent ability at the plate. These titles came in 1961, 1964, 1965 and 1967.

- **All-Star Game**. Clemente was selected for the MLB All-Star Game 15 times during his career. Each selection allowed him to showcase his talent to a national audience, and he often responded with outstanding performances.

- **Homerun in crucial situations**. Clemente hit numerous home runs in high-pressure situations during his career, sending Pirates fans into a frenzy.

- **12 Gold Gloves as a right fielder**. Clemente won the Gold Glove as a right fielder for 12 consecutive seasons from 1961 to 1972. This award shows his outstanding defensive skills and ability to make spectacular plays on the field.

- **MVP of the National League in 1966**.

- **1971 World Series**. Clemente performed excellently during the 1971 World Series against the Baltimore Orioles. He had a .414 batting average during the series, leading the Pittsburgh Pirates to victory. His performance earned him the World Series MVP award.

- **3,000 Hit**. The most iconic moment in Clemente's career is when he got his 3,000th valid hit on September 30th, 1972. It was the last hit of his regular career and solidified his place in baseball history.

- **The last game was in 1972**. Clemente's last match in 1972, although known to be the game in which he reached his 3,000th valid, was emotional for many fans, as no one knew it would be the last time they would see him play.

- **Defensive plays**. Clemente was known for his offensive skills and was among the most talented right fielders ever. He was known for his accurate and robust right-field throws, often getting runners out at home or third base. These extraordinary plays often sent fans into a frenzy.

- **Multiple-value games**. Clemente could take control of games with his bat. He had matches with three or four valid hits on several occasions, fueling the crowd's enthusiasm.

- **His jersey number**, No. 21, was retired by the Pittsburgh Pirates.

- **"Hall of Fame"**. In 1973, he was inducted into Baseball's "Hall of Fame" under a special waiver that bypassed the usual five-year waiting period.

- **MLB also established the *"Roberto Clemente Award"***. Awarded annually to the player who best represents the game of baseball through outstanding character, community involvement, philanthropy, and contributions on and off the field.

Although this is not a specific *"moment"* there were occasions when even fans of opposing teams applauded Clemente's exploits on the field, recognizing his mastery and talent.

Clemente was known for his compassion, honesty, and commitment to improving the living conditions of the less fortunate. He contributed to many charitable initiatives and always tried to return what he had received from life to the world.
Despite his many achievements and accolades, Clemente remained humble.

He always put others before himself and saw his position as a platform to do good. Clemente felt he had a responsibility to his community and to humanity at large. This notion of duty can inspire young people to look for ways to contribute positively to their community or the world, regardless of their field of interest or profession.

Even in the face of challenges, Clemente's determination to help others teaches the importance of resilience. His story can inspire others to persevere in adversity and look for ways to overcome obstacles. Clemente was genuine in his humanitarian efforts.
He was not in it for fame or glory.

Dedicating time and energy to helping others can lead to a deep sense of accomplishment. Clemente's story can inspire others to seek those opportunities, recognizing giving can often be more rewarding than receiving.

COMPASSION

Is the empathic ability to perceive, recognize, and respond to the pain and suffering of others, accompanied by a sincere desire to alleviate such suffering. It goes beyond simple understanding or empathy: compassion prompts action, motivating one to help and support those in distress. It is a fundamental human trait which connects people through love, kindness, and solidarity, fostering deep relationships and a sense of community.

Chapter 4

BABE RUTH
THE GIANT OF AMERICAN BASEBALL

In the early days of baseball, when stadium lights were not yet so bright and jerseys not so shiny, a giant walked among the men. This giant's name was Babe Ruth, however to the world, he was known as *"The Kid"*.

Immersed in the atmosphere of an America in turmoil, Babe Ruth changed forever the way baseball was played and perceived. It was not just the power of his home runs that left the audience breathless, but the infectious charisma and sheer joy with which he played.

When Babe was on the field, every game became an event, every act a work of art, and every swing an emotion.

But Babe was not just a burst of talent on the diamond.

Off the field, he was known for his big heart and even bigger personality. He didn't just care about scoring runs or breaking records; he cared about people. With his infectious smile and thunderous laugh, Babe had the ability to bring people together, making baseball accessible and loved by millions.

He was a man who not only knew how to play, he knew how to live.

He lived every moment to the fullest, whether it was a decisive hit in a World Series or a laugh with children in a hospital. Babe Ruth embodied the American dream: a boy with humble beginnings who, through talent, determination, and a dash of daring, became a legend.

If there is anything you should learn from Babe Ruth, it is greatness is not only defined by the successes you achieve, it also includes the way you influence the lives of others.

Babe was not just a baseball player; he was a phenomenon, a pioneer, and most importantly, an eternal example of how passion, talent, and a golden heart can change the world. May his spirit and story inspire you to find your passion, follow your heart and become the best version of yourself.

George Herman "*Babe*" Ruth Jr. was born on February 6th, 1895, in Baltimore, Maryland. His childhood was not easy, on the contrary can be considered turbulent. Babe Ruth was one of eight children born to Kate Schamberger-Ruth and George Herman Ruth Sr. although only he and his younger sister, Mamie, survived childhood. His father was a bartender and ran several breweries in Baltimore. Ruth often found himself in trouble during his youth. He was known to skip school, cause minor problems, and cause problems for his parents. Because of his restless and undisciplined behavior, he was sent at the age of 7 to St. Mary's Industrial School for Boys, primarily and orphanage and boarding school, run by Xaverian friars, where the children contributed to the care of the facility, learn trades, and became productive.

There he spent most of his youth and adolescence. It was at St. Mary's that Ruth was introduced to baseball. Brother Matthias, one of the friars at the institute, noticed Ruth's natural talent for the game. Matthias became a paternal figure to Ruth, encouraging and coaching him in baseball. Under his guidance, Ruth developed his skills as both a pitcher and a hitter.

At the age of 19, after spending most of his life at St. Mary's, Babe Ruth was noticed by Jack Dunn, owner and manager of the Baltimore Orioles, a minor league team. Dunn was so impressed with Ruth's talent that he took him under his wing and signed him to the team. It was Dunn who gave him the nickname *"Babe"*. Soon after, Ruth was sold to the Boston Red Sox, where he would begin his legendary career in Major League Baseball.

The humble origins and hardships of his youth influenced in part the person he became, both as a player and as a man. His resilience, innate talent and the guidance he received during his formative years at St. Mary's helped shape one of the greatest baseball players of all times. Babe Ruth was one of the most charismatic and dominant baseball players ever.

During his career, there were many moments when Babe sent the audience into ecstasy.

- **Babe Ruth's First Day at Fenway**. On July 11th, 1914, Ruth made his MLB debut with the Boston Red Sox. Although he did not bat during the game, simply seeing him take the field was already a sign of what was to come.

- **His first career home run**. Ruth hit his first home run in the MLB on May 6th, 1915, while playing for the Boston Red Sox against the New York Yankees. This was just the beginning of his legendary career as a hitter.

- **Outfield in the 1916 World Series**. Although he was primarily a pitcher at that time, Ruth showed his skills as a hitter by hitting a decisive home run during the 1916 World Series.

- **Home run record in the 1919 season**. In 1919, even before his historic 60 home run season of 1927,

Ruth had already broken the record for home runs in a season with 29, sending fans into a frenzy and anticipating his future greatness as a hitter.

- **Sale to the New York Yankees**. In 1920, Ruth was sold to the New York Yankees. During his first season with the Yankees, he set a new MLB record with 54 home runs, surpassing his previous record of 29.

- **1927 season**. Ruth, along with Lou Gehrig, led the *"Murderers Row"* Yankees to one of the most dominant seasons in baseball history. That year, Ruth set a new MLB record with 60 home runs in a season, a record which would last for 34 years.

- **1928 World Series**. Ruth hit three home runs in a single World Series game, delighting the crowd and leading the Yankees to victory.

- **"Called Shot" of 1932**. During the third game of the 1932 World Series against the Chicago Cubs, Ruth is said to have *"called"* his shot, indicating where he would hit the home run. Then, with the count at two strikes, Ruth hit a home run at the exact spot he had indicated, sending the Wrigley Field crowd and spectators across the country into a frenzy.

- **Performance in Japan**. In 1934, Ruth was part of a team of MLB stars which toured Japan. His performances there, including some impressive home runs, electrified Japanese audiences and helped cement his fame internationally.

- **Last appearance as a Yankee**. On September 30th, 1934, Babe Ruth donned the Yankees uniform for the last time. Although he was clearly at the end of his career, his last appearance as a Yankee was an emotional and memorable moment for fans.

- **Last home run**. On May 25th, 1935, playing for the Boston Braves, Ruth hit home runs numbers 712,

713 and 714, his last major league bases. His 714th home run was a spectacular hit that thrilled the crowd.

- **Home Run Record**. Babe Ruth, throughout his career, set the record for the most home runs in a single season multiple times. Although this record was later surpassed, his skill changed the way baseball was viewed, shifting the focus to the attacking game and the importance of home runs.

Advice from the Heart of the Diamond

The stadium was shrouded in pregnant silence, with only the dull sound of stadium lights humming in the air. Shadows danced across the playing field, revealing a legendary figure and a young man, their bodies almost tangential.

"*Babe*", said the young man, his eyes bright and his gaze full of hope mixed with awe, "***I don't know if I can do it. Every time I take the field, I feel the weight of all those expectations on me***". Babe Ruth, with his infectious smile and a presence which could fill an entire stadium, put a heavy hand on the boy's shoulder. "*Son*", he said in a deep voice, "***I'm going to tell you something I've learned over the years. Baseball... well, it's not just a game. It's life. And in life, there will always be expectations, pressures, and times when you feel overwhelmed***".
The boy swallowed, trying to absorb the legend's words.

Babe laughed softly, "***Who said it was easy? I've had my struggles, my fears. But the key is to love what you do, passionately. You have to believe in yourself, even when it seems like the whole world is doubting you***".

"But what if I'm wrong?" the boy asked, almost in a whisper. *"You will be wrong"*, Babe replied without hesitation. *"You will fail, you will make mistakes. But it is from those mistakes that you will learn and grow. I never hit every ball thrown my way, but I always tried to learn from every pitch, every mistake"*.

The boy stared at Babe, the intensity of the moment enveloping them both.

AUTHENTICITY

Is the quality of being true, sincere and in harmony with one's essence, having overcome conditioning and trauma. It manifests itself through being consistent with one's values, thoughts, feelings and actions, without wearing masks or trying to conform to others' expectations. An authentic person is not afraid to show his or her true nature, with its strengths and vulnerabilities. Authenticity promotes genuine relationships, mutual trust and self-esteem because it is based on sincerity and the integrity of being oneself in all circumstances.

Chapter 5

JIM ABBOTT
MASTER OF SELF-ESTEEM ON THE DIAMOND

I n the history of sports, few stories are as inspiring and feature human tenacity as the story of Jim Abbott. Abbott was not just a talented baseball player. He was a living symbol of overcoming and resilience.

Jim Abbott was born in 1967 without the right hand.

Most people would have considered this an insurmountable challenge to pursuing a career in baseball, a sport which depends critically on hand coordination. However, Abbott not only played baseball, he excelled, reaching the pinnacle of his sport: Major League Baseball (MLB).

Being born without a hand is more than just a physical difference, it is an ongoing interaction between the individual and a world designed for those with two hands.

It is a dynamic between fitting in and being different, a balance that is far from easy to meet.

Imagine what it is like to grow up in a society which often, consciously or unconsciously, values a certain idea of "*normalcy*".

Every glance, every whisper from strangers can give rise to issues of self-esteem. In this context, the perception of one's own worth can become unstable ground, particularly during adolescence, a period already fraught with insecurities. The individual may begin to wonder, "*Where do I fit in? Will I ever be accepted for who I am?*"

And then there are the social challenges. Children can be ruthlessly honest, but sometimes cruel. Innocent questions from peers about the lack of a helping hand can evolve into marginalization or, worse, bullying.

Under these circumstances, the temptation to withdraw, to avoid social situations, may grow. But it is also in these moments of difficulty deep and meaningful connections can be found.

For some people understanding and acceptance can have a profound impact, helping to build lifelong resilience.

People with a physical difference often develop an incredible ability to adapt. The skills they acquire are not only physical, but also psychological.

Resilience, the ability to overcome obstacles and see beyond one's challenges, becomes second nature. This inner strength can become a source of inspiration for everyone around them.

Life without a hand, or any other physical difference, is a complex journey of challenges and triumphs. But as is often the case, it is through the greatest challenges the most beautiful stories of determination, courage and humanity emerge.

Because of his impairment from the moment he began playing baseball as a child, Abbott has had to find innovative ways to compensate.

With a custom baseball glove, he developed a technique in which he would throw the ball and then quickly move the glove to his left hand, preparing for action.

It wasn't just a trick; it was a demonstration of his determination to overcome any obstacle.

His career at the University of Michigan was extraordinary, culminating in winning the gold medal for baseball at the 1988 Olympic Games. However Abbott did not stop there. He was chosen eighth overall in the 1988 MLB draft by the California Angels and made his MLB debut the following year.

The highlight of his career came in 1993 when, playing for the New York Yankees, Abbott threw a no-hitter against the Cleveland Indians. An extraordinary feat for any pitcher. For Abbott, it was a demonstration of how well he could overcome challenges.

Jim Abbott's story is not just one of a successful athlete. It is one of a man who refused to let circumstances define his limitations. He turned what many would have seen as a disability into a source of strength, inspiring countless individuals along the way.

Abbott showed the world with determination, grit and a positive mindset, challenges can not only be met, they can be overcome. His story remains a glowing reminder that human potential has no limits, no matter what challenges life presents.

Letter from Jim Abbott

"There is a feeling I know all too well, that of looking in the mirror and seeing something the world might call imperfect. But let me tell you something, young friend.

What you see as an obstacle can become your greatest strength. When I was a child, my lack was evident.

*But instead of letting it define me, I chose to define myself. Whenever someone told me I couldn't do something, I used those words as fuel. **Every "you can't" became a "look at how I do it"**. I know there will be times when* *you feel that the world is against you. But in those moments, remember that your diversity is a gift.*

It is a unique perspective, a strength that many do not possess. Your challenges shape you, but they do not define you. **Dream big, don't beat yourself up, and above all, believe in yourself. Don't compare yourself to others, but aspire to become the best version of yourself.** *And when doubt assails you, think of me, a boy born without a hand who pitched a no-hitter in the MLB. Not because I was special, but because I refused to listen to doubt and chose to listen to my heart.*

If there is one piece of advice I would like to give you, it is this: never let the world tell you who you are or what you can do. **You are the master of your destiny. Struggle, dream, love and, above all, live with passion. Your "imperfection" could be the key that opens the door to your greatest adventures".**

With love and hope". Jim Abbott.

SELF ESTEEM

Is an individual's evaluation and appreciation of himself or herself. It refers to the perception of one's worth and competence in various areas of life. Healthy self-esteem involves recognizing and accepting both one's strengths and weaknesses, and having a balanced and positive view of oneself, regardless of outside opinions or circumstances. Self-esteem affects how we behave, how we face challenges, and how we react and make decisions. Strong self-esteem is fundamental to psychological well-being.

Chapter 6

LOU GEHRIG
REAL LUCK IN LIFE

Lou Gehrig, known to be one of the greatest baseball players in history, began his remarkable sports career from humble beginnings and with an innate passion for baseball from his youth in New York City.

Born June 19th, 1903, in the Yorkville neighborhood on the east side of Manhattan, Gehrig grew up in a family of German descent. His father, Heinrich Gehrig, was a worker in a railroad shop, and his mother, Christina Fack, was a housewife. Lou was their only child, and the family lived in a modest apartment. From an early age, Lou Gehrig showed an early interest in sports, particularly baseball. The city streets were his makeshift playgrounds, and he spent hours throwing and hitting balls against brick walls or in makeshift playgrounds in local parks.

His passion was evident from his early years, and he was encouraged by his parents to pursue his dream. The turning point in his young career came when he began playing baseball at the high school level. Lou Gehrig attended George Washington High School in the Washington Heights neighborhood of Manhattan, where he played on the school's baseball team. His extraordinary ability to hit the ball and his dexterity at first base soon made him a star in the world of youth baseball. After completing high school, Gehrig received a scholarship to attend Columbia University, where he continued to cultivate his talent for baseball. At Columbia, Gehrig distinguished himself as a baseball player and became a prominent figure on the university team. His power in hitting the ball and his defensive ability at first base attracted the attention of scouts from professional baseball teams.

It was during his time at Columbia that Gehrig caught the attention of the New York Yankees, one of MLB's most prestigious teams. In 1923, while still a college student, Gehrig signed a contract with the Yankees, thus beginning his professional career.

Here are some of Lou Gehrig's most memorable moments and major accomplishments.

- **2,130 consecutive appearances**. One of the most iconic moments in Gehrig's career was the record number of consecutive games played, a streak which lasted over 14 years. This incredible length in the New York Yankees lineup became a symbol of his extraordinary stamina and dedication to the game.

- **Four-out game**. On June 3rd, 1932, Lou Gehrig accomplished one of the most extraordinary feats in baseball history by hitting four home runs in a single game against the Detroit Tigers. This feat has remained in history as one of baseball's most incredible and electrifying moments.

- **World Series victories**. Lou Gehrig won six World Series titles with the New York Yankees during his career. These victories captured the imagination of fans and solidified his reputation as one of the best players of all time.

- **MVP Awards**. Gehrig was awarded the American League MVP title twice, in 1927 and 1936. These awards testify to his consistent excellence in game and his significant contributions to the team.

- **Farewell speech**. On July 4th, 1939, Lou Gehrig gave an emotional and touching farewell speech at Yankee Stadium, announcing his retirement from baseball due to the disease that now bears his name, amyotrophic lateral sclerosis (ALS). This moment has remained in the public imagination as one of the most moving moments in sports history.

- **Induction into the *"Hall of Fame"***. In 1939, the same year of his retirement, Lou Gehrig was one of the first five players to be inducted into the *"National Baseball Hall of Fame"*.

- **Impressive career numbers**. By the end of his career, Lou Gehrig had amassed extraordinary statistics, including a .340 batting average, 493 home runs and 1,995 runs batted in.

Imagine a sunny day at a baseball field, with an enthusiastic crowd erupting with joy as an imposing figure steps up to the plate. It is Lou Gehrig, known by the nickname *"The Iron Horse"* for his extraordinary stamina in the game.

There is something deeper in those eyes and words. Gehrig teaches us in life, much like baseball, gratitude takes center stage.

He begins his speech, and his eyes reveal an inner world. *"I've been called The Iron Horse", but let me tell you something: It's not the number of consecutive games I've played that really matters"*.

Gehrig emphasizes that even in the most unexpected challenges, such as the disease which would later bear his name, gratitude finds its place. *"Life threw me an unexpected ball, but even in the midst of that storm, I found gratitude"*, he says.

"When I said I considered myself the luckiest man on the face of the earth, I wasn't talking about my accomplishments on the baseball field. I was talking about every moment, every laugh, every person I met, every challenge I faced".

"Remember, real luck is not found in trophies or records. It is found in the heart, in the ability to appreciate every moment, every challenge, every opportunity. This is the message I want you to carry with you".

GRATITUDE

What exactly is it? Gratitude is a special way of looking at the world, in which you recognize and appreciate the good things in your life. It is like saying "Thank you!" to the world for everything it offers you, good or bad. It is the recognition and appreciation for the positive things, people and experiences in your life. We should all feel gratitude even for experiences that we judge to be negative since through these we evolve and grow much more. It is a state of mind which focuses on abundance rather than shortage, and on blessings rather than deprivation. Expressing gratitude means not only giving thanks for great deeds or achievements, yet also recognizing and appreciating small moments and daily kindnesses. Regular practice of gratitude can improve emotional well-being, strengthen relationships and increase satisfaction in life. Being grateful helps to have a more positive outlook, promoting a sense of abundance and happiness.

Gratitude is like a magic wand that turns every day into an extraordinary adventure.

Gratitude is:
- Like a happy pill. When you begin to recognize the positive things in your life, you begin to feel happier. Even on gray days, you will find a reason to smile.
- Your super-anti-stress. It helps you reduce anxiety and nervousness, giving you a feeling of inner calm. Imagine facing exams or stressful situations with a smile on your face!
- A magical glue which strengthens your relationships. When you show appreciation toward others, you create stronger and more solid bonds. People will love you even more.
- An inexhaustible source of energy. It gives you the strength to overcome challenges and pursue your dreams. There is nothing you can't do when you are charged with gratitude!
- The best way to focus on what you have. Gratitude helps you stop fixating on what you don't have and appreciate what you do have. It makes you see the resources and opportunities you already have.
- Medicine for the spirit. Some research suggests it can improve your mental and physical health by lowering blood pressure and increasing resistance to pain.
- Contagious. When you start practicing it, you inspire others to do it, too. You can spread happiness wherever you go!
Gratitude is the secret key to an extraordinary life!

Chapter 7

KIRK GIBSON
THE KING OF IMPOSSIBLE HOMERUNS

I want to tell you one of the most extraordinary and inspiring stories in the world of baseball: the impossible home run of Kirk Gibson.

This is a tale of tenacity, determination, and the ability to overcome any obstacle. Get ready to be inspired!

It was October 15th, 1988, and the Los Angeles Dodgers were struggling.

They were in the finals of the World Series against the mighty Oakland Athletics. Gibson, one of the team's stars, was badly injured in his leg and had difficulty even walking, let alone running or playing baseball. When the game reached the ninth inning and the Dodgers were down by one run, it seemed defeat was inevitable. But there was one thing no one had considered: the unyielding determination of Kirk Gibson.

With his face contracted in pain and his left leg severely compromised, Gibson stepped up to the plate to face one of the league's most feared pitchers, Dennis Eckersley.

Everyone knew it was nearly impossible, but Gibson had no intention of giving up.

Gibson hit a home run. Not just any home run, but an incredible, miraculous hit which sent the ball well over the fence. As he staggered along the bases, with the crowd in a frenzy, it went down in history as one of the most iconic moments in baseball.

But this home run was more than just a hit. It was the evidence of Gibson's perseverance, his willingness to fight against all odds and never give up. It is a symbol of the strength of the human spirit and what can be accomplished when you have the determination to overcome obstacles. So the next time you are faced with a challenge, think of Kirk Gibson and his impossible home run. With determination and perseverance, you can overcome any obstacle and achieve success!

Kirk Gibson was born on May 28th, 1957, in Pontiac, Michigan, United States. He grew up in a baseball-loving family and began playing baseball at a young age. He attended Waterford Kettering High School, where he showed considerable talent in baseball and football.

Gibson was named an All American.

What does that mean? Being named an All-American means the player has demonstrated exceptional ability in his sport. This ability can be demonstrated through outstanding and consistent performance over time on the field.

All-American players often have a significant impact on their team's success. Their skills help advance the team in competition and can be a key part of their success.

In 1978, Kirk Gibson was selected in the first round of the MLB draft by the Detroit Tigers. He made his major league debut with the Tigers in 1979 and quickly became an important part of the team. He continued to play for the Tigers until 1987.

Subsequently, Gibson played for several major league teams, including the Los Angeles Dodgers, Kansas City Royals, and Oakland Athletics. Kirk Gibson officially announced his retirement from MLB as a professional player after the 1995 season, and pursued a career as a baseball coach and manager.

His legacy as a baseball player remains one of the most important in the history of the game.

His career was marked by moments of great success, but also by challenges and injuries.

- **The Home Run in the 1985 All-Star Game**. Gibson was selected to represent the American League in the 1985 All-Star Game. During the game, he hit a home run which was one of the highlights of the event.

- **Gibson's Cycle in 1985**. In 1985, Gibson became the second player in Detroit Tigers history to accomplish the cycle (hitting a single, a double, a triple and a home run in a single game). This rare achievement was a significant moment in his career.

- **Home run in the 1986 All-Star Game**. In 1986, Gibson was again selected to represent the American League in the All-Star Game. During the game, he hit a home run which contributed to his team's success.

- **Gibson's home run in the 1988 National League Championship Series**. Before his famous home run in the 1988 World Series, Gibson hit a home run in the National League Championship Series against the New York Mets.

- **The 1988 All-Star Game home run**. In 1988, Gibson represented the American League in the All-Star Game. In the ninth inning, with his team trailing, he hit a decisive home run against the National League's top pitcher, Dwight Gooden. This moment of play was a flash of brilliance and demonstrated Gibson's talent even in high-pressure situations.

- **The Impossible Outfield of the 1988 World Series**. This is probably the most iconic moment of Kirk Gibson's career. During the 1988 World Series, when he was playing for the Los Angeles Dodgers, Gibson was badly injured in his leg and was not even expected to be in the lineup. However, with his team down and two outs in the ninth inning of the first game of the World Series, he was inserted as a hitter. He hit a game-winning home run despite his precarious physical state, giving the Dodgers an epic victory.

- **The Grand Slam in Game 5 of the 1988 National League Championship Series**. In Game 5 of the 1988 NLCS against the New York Mets, Gibson hit a grand slam that contributed to the Dodgers' victory. This key performance propelled the Dodgers to the World Series.

- **The home run on Opening Day 1989**. Gibson began his 1989 season with a home run on Opening Day against the Atlanta Braves, an exciting moment for Dodgers fans.

- **The Cycle in 1989**. During his 1989 season with the Los Angeles Dodgers, Gibson completed another cycle, demonstrating his versatility as a player.

- **The Comeback Outfield in 1991**. After moving to the Kansas City Royals in 1991, Gibson hit a home run in his first at bat of the season, once again demonstrating his strength and talent as a hitter.

- **The home run in the 1995 National League Championship Series**. In 1995, playing for the Kansas City Royals, Gibson hit a home run in the

NLCS against the Cleveland Indians. This home run was a major contributor to the Royals' victory in the series.

- **The Comeback Home Run in 2000**. After his retirement from baseball, Kirk Gibson made a special appearance in a charity game in 2000. In his first turn at bat, he hit a home run, showing even after retiring, he still had the magic touch.

- **His Stolen Base Record**. Although Gibson was best known for his power hitting, he also proved to be an aggressive runner. In 1985, he set a record for stolen bases for the Tigers with 29.

His entire competitive career is a testimony of Gibson's perseverance, his willingness to fight against all odds and never give up. He is a symbol of the strength of the human spirit and what can be accomplished when you have the determination to overcome obstacles. When you are faced with a challenge, think of Kirk Gibson and his impossible home run. With determination and perseverance, you can overcome any obstacle and achieve success!

DETERMINATION

Is the firm will and resolve to pursue goals or overcome challenges, despite obstacles, adversity or distractions. It is the inner strength which drives an individual to continue and persist, even when circumstances become difficult or seem adverse. A determined person is focused, tenacious and not easily discouraged.

Determination is often what distinguishes those who achieve their goals from those who give up in the face of difficulties. It is a key trait for success in any field because it motivates one to stay committed and take that extra step necessary to achieve one's aspirations.

Chapter 8

JOE DI MAGGIO
HERO OF 56 JOKES

Joe Di Maggio, nicknamed *"The Yankee Clipper"*, is one of the most iconic players in baseball history and, in particular, of the New York Yankees.

Born in 1914 in Martinez, California, Di Maggio was the son of Italian immigrants. His father, Giuseppe, was a fisherman from Sicily and worked in San Francisco Bay.

Di Maggio grew up in a family of nine children, and although baseball was his passion, he initially worked with his father in fishing boats. The family's expectations were that he would follow in his father's footsteps, but Joe had other plans.

Di Maggio began his professional baseball career with the San Francisco Seals, a Pacific Coast League team, in 1932. During his time with the Seals, he established a streak of 61 games with at least one valid hit.

In 1936, Di Maggio made his Major Leagues debut with the New York Yankees. During his career, he became known not only for his extraordinary ability in the field, but also for his professionalism and reserved attitude. His streak of 56 games with at least one run in 1941 is considered one of baseball's most elusive records.

He married Hollywood legend Marilyn Monroe, although their marriage was turbulent and short-lived. Despite his fame and achievements, Di Maggio remained known for his reserve and humility.

His career was interrupted by World War II, during which he served in the Armed Forces. However, upon his return, he continued to play at a high level until his retirement in 1951.

Di Maggio spent the rest of his life away from the limelight, retiring to Florida, where he died in 1999. His legacy as one of the greatest baseball players of all time endures, and his story is an example of dedication, humility and love for the game.

Joe Di Maggio, one of the greatest baseball players of all time, had numerous significant moments in his career which touched the hearts of fans and sports fans deeply.

- **Rookie Sensation**. In his rookie year in 1936, Di Maggio helped the Yankees win the World Series. His immediate presence and impact on the field deeply impressed fans.

- **World Series streak**. Di Maggio played for the Yankees during a period of dominance in Major League Baseball. He helped lead the team to victory in the World Series in four consecutive years, from 1936 to 1939.

- **The 56-Game Streak**. The streak of 56 consecutive games with at least one valid hit in 1941 is one of baseball's most celebrated records. During this period, anticipation and excitement built with each game, with fans and media paying attention to Di Maggio's every turn at bat.

- **Return from Military Service**. Like many athletes of the era, DiMaggio served in the armed forces during World War II. His return to baseball in 1946 was greeted with great enthusiasm and gratitude from the fans.

- **All-Star Game**. Di Maggio was selected for the MLB All-Star Game 13 times during his career. Each selection was a celebration of his abilities and a proud moment for Yankees fans

- **The Last Game**. The retirement game of a great athlete is always emotional, and Di Maggio's in 1951 was no different. Fans of the Yankees and all of baseball paid tribute to him for his extraordinary career.

- **The Death of Marilyn Monroe**. Although he was not closely associated with baseball, Di Maggio's deep connection with Hollywood icon Marilyn Monroe attracted the world's attention. After Monroe's death in 1962, DiMaggio, her ex-husband, arranged the funeral and for decades sent roses to her grave site. His posthumous dedication to Monroe touched many.

- **The return to Monument Park**. In 1969, Di Maggio was honored by the Yankees when his number, 5, was retired and his name added to Monument Park at Yankee Stadium. The ceremony was a moving tribute to his legendary career with the Yankees.

- **Mr. Coffee commercial**. Although it may seem minor compared to other moments in his sports career, Di Maggio also became a familiar face in American homes as a testimonial for Mr. Coffee in the 1970s and 1980s. His presence in these commercials made him recognizable even to generations who had not seen him play.

- **Strip 50th Anniversary Speech**. In 1991, Di Maggio was honored at Yankee Stadium to commemorate the 50th anniversary of his 56-game hitting streak. During the event, he gave a speech before thousands of fans who had come to celebrate his historic record.

- **The Tribute in 1999**. When DiMaggio died in 1999, the sports world paid tribute to one of its greatest icons. The New York Yankees wore his number, 5, on their uniforms for the entire season, and there were numerous tributes across the country.

Di Maggio's stature as a sports and cultural figure in the United States ensured many moments in his life and career were observed and commemorated by fans, journalists, and baseball fans.

Time for a beer together

As the dim lights of the bar draw shadows on the wooden table, you find yourself sitting next to a legend, Joe DiMaggio. The cold beer in your hand contrasts with the warmth of the room, and there is a palpable anticipation in the air. Anticipation not for what will be said, but for what will be shared.

With a slight sigh, Di Maggio begins, *"Many people think that the life of an athlete is just about talent. But there's something deeper, something that burns inside and pushes you to go beyond all limits"*.

His fingers play with the glass, reflections of lights dance on the golden liquid. *"This flame, this inner fire, is passion. It's what woke me up every morning, what drove me to perfect every movement, every swing, every pitch. But it's not just in baseball, it's in life. Find what makes you feel alive and pursue it with all of yourself".*

You lean back, savoring every word. There is a depth in his eyes, a history of challenges faced, victories and defeats. *"But in your quest for excellence, never forget who you are. I have seen many lose it all, swept away by the illusion of fame or the lure of money. Your integrity, your essence, is the compass that will guide you through the storms".*

Time seems to expand, and every second shared with this legend feels like a gift. *"I had my moments of doubt. Moments when the pressure seemed unbearable. But each time, I searched within myself, remembered where I came from and who I was. And that knowledge, that inner truth, has been my anchor".*

As the conversation unravels, you realize you are not just listening to the tale of a baseball champion, rather the wise reflections of a man who has gone through decades of change, challenges and triumphs. And in his story, you see reflected your own dreams, hopes and fears. With a grateful smile, you raise your glass in a silent toast, to Joe Di Maggio, and all the valuable lessons life has to offer.

The fundamental lesson which emerges from Joe Di Maggio's words and life, from how we might imagine it through this account, is the synergy between passion and integrity. Passion is what fuels the ardor, determination, and desire to excel at what we love. However at the same time, passion without integrity can lead us astray.

Integrity serves as a compass, keeping us grounded in our core values and ensuring we do not get lost in the tumult of fame, success or the expectations of others.

Di Maggio's teaching can be summarized as, *"**Pursue what you love with all your heart, but never lose sight of who you really are**"*.

BEING ONESELF

Implies living in authenticity, acting and expressing yourself in a manner consistent with your essence, values and feelings, regardless of external expectations or pressures. It means accepting and embracing one's uniqueness, strengths, vulnerabilities and imperfections, without trying to conform to an ideal image or to fit what society deems acceptable. Being oneself is the key to living an authentic and meaningful life, as it allows one to build genuine relationships, make decisions in line with one's true self, and experience an inner freedom resulting from sincerity and consistency.

Chapter 9

MO'NE DAVIS
BASEBALL IS ALSO WOMEN'S

M o'ne Davis hails from the bustling city of Philadelphia, Pennsylvania.
Her youth in Philadelphia, with its vibrant streets and rich sports history, played a key role in shaping her passion for baseball.

Growing up in a community where sports were seen as a means of expression and escape, Mo'ne learned early on the importance of determination and hard work. Her family, while aware of the challenges she might face as a girl in a male-dominated sport, has always supported and encouraged her to follow her dreams.

However, it is not just a matter of geographical origin.

The environment in which she grew up, the people who influenced her, and the challenges she faced in the streets and fields of Philadelphia all helped shape her resilient character and worldview. Her background is not just a place or an environment; it is a combination of experiences, relationships, and life lessons that have helped her become the athlete and person she is today.

Mo'ne has experienced many important sports Moments.

- **Winning Game at LLWS.** The moment that truly made history was when Mo'ne became the first girl to pitch a winning game in the Little League World Series. Her performance showed the world that talent and passion know no gender, and the stands were in a frenzy for her.

- **Home Run at LLWS.** Mo'ne didn't just shine as a pitcher. She also hit a home run during the tournament, another moment when the audience swooned.

- **Sports Illustrated cover.** Shortly after her success at LLWS, Mo'ne Davis was the cover star of Sports Illustrated. Being so young and already on one of the most prestigious covers in the sports world raised a wave of excitement and admiration.

- **NBA All-Star Celebrity Match.** Mo'ne also demonstrated her basketball skills. During a celebrity game in the NBA All-Star Weekend, she dribbled Kevin Hart, a moment which divided social media and showed her versatility as an athlete.

Her pitching ability, particularly her devastating changeup pitch, stunned many opposing hitters and made her emerge as one of the bright stars of the tournament. She not only challenged and broke gender barriers in baseball, but also inspired countless young female athletes around the world.

In absolute terms of performance in baseball, there are players who have achieved more at the professional level. However, what makes Mo'ne Davis's accomplishments remarkable and impressive is the context in which they were achieved.

Baseball, especially in youth leagues such as the Little League World Series, has historically been dominated by males. Mo'ne defied prevailing expectations by becoming the first girl to achieve certain results in the tournament. This alone has great significance, considering the cultural and social barriers girls and women face in sports.

Mo'ne was only 13 years old when she made history in the LLWS.

At so young an age, managing the pressure and expectations of the public, media, and peers, especially on an international platform, is an accomplishment in itself.

Beyond her performance on the field, Mo'ne's impact transcends baseball. She has inspired countless well-rounded girls, showing they can compete and succeed in any traditionally male-dominated field. Her story has had a social impact, challenging traditional perceptions and encouraging a new generation of female athletes.

Mo'ne Davis, with her slender stature and determined eyes, walked the pitcher's mound. She was not there just to play; she was there to prove something. Every pitch, every movement, spoke of a burning desire to challenge an ingrained prejudice at the heart of American baseball: that the diamond was a place for boys, and girls were out of place.

With every pitch she threw, Mo'ne not only sent opposing batters out, she silently challenged the expectations of an entire nation. One could almost feel the weight of prejudice crumbling with each strike. Whispers of surprise turned into shouts of encouragement. *"She's a girl!"*, some exclaimed. *"And she's dominating!"*

But for Mo'ne, it wasn't just about winning games or making history. It was about proving passion and talent know no gender. That a girl can throw, bat, run and compete with the same intensity and skill as any boy. That prejudice can be overcome, not with words, rather with decisive action and heart.

The message was clear: ***the baseball field belongs to anyone with the courage to dream and the determination to pursue those dreams, regardless of gender***. And as Mo'ne left the field, she knew she had done something bigger than herself. She had ignited a flame of hope and inspiration, proving barriers exist only as long as we allow them to exist.

FIGHTING AGAINST PREJUDGES

Means actively opposing pre-packaged ideas and judgments that are made about individuals or groups based on stereotypes rather than hard facts or direct experience. These judgments, often rooted in deep cultural, historical or social traditions, may relate to race, gender, sexual orientation, religion, social class, age, disability, among others.

Fighting prejudice requires becoming informed and gaining a deeper understanding of people and cultures that are traditionally victims of prejudice, breaking the silence, and promoting diversity.

Fighting prejudice is not only a matter of social justice; it is also a way to enrich one's life by welcoming a wider range of experiences, stories and perspectives. In an increasingly globalized and interconnected world, this struggle is critical to building cohesive, inclusive and prosperous communities.

Chapter 10

JACKIE ROBINSON
BEYOND THE DIAMOND FOR TRUE EQUALITY

Have you ever heard of a hero who wore a baseball uniform? Well, sit back and let me tell you the story of Jackie Robinson, a man whose courage and determination transformed the world of baseball and beyond.

Once upon a time, many years ago, there were teams on which you could not play if you had skin of a certain color. Can you imagine what it felt like to be excluded from something you love just because of the color of your skin? Jackie knew what it felt like, but he did not give in to the prejudices of his time. With a bat, a glove, and a big heart, he set out to show the world anyone, regardless of skin color, can become a star.

Every time he took the field, he heard the cries and protests of many who did not want him to play. But with the courage of a lion, Jackie kept playing, running faster, throwing and batting with all his might, proving to everyone a true champion is found inside, in the heart, and not on the skin.

His story is not only about baseball, but it teaches us we can overcome any obstacle and change the world around us with determination and courage, So the next time you see a baseball field, remember Jackie Robinson, the hero who changed the game and showed everyone what it really means to be a champion.

Jackie Roosevelt Robinson was born on January 31st, 1919, in Cairo, Georgia.

He was the youngest of five children. His family was of African American descent and lived in the segregated Deep South.

After his father abandoned the family, Jackie's mother, Mallie Robinson, decided to move with her five children to Pasadena, California, where she hoped to find better opportunities for her family. Here Robinson grew up in a less segregated environment than in the South, but still faced the challenges of racism.

Robinson attended Pasadena Junior College, where he excelled in many sports, including football, basketball, track and field, and baseball. After Pasadena JC, he transferred to the University of California, Los Angeles (UCLA), becoming the first athlete in the university's history to win "*varsity letters*" in four sports. "*Varsity letters*" are awards given in the United States for excellence in sports and school activities. They are badges or patches, usually in the shape of a letter, representing the athlete's school or college.

During World War II, Robinson was drafted into the U.S. Army, where he attained the rank of second lieutenant.

During his service he faced discrimination and was tried (and later acquitted) for insubordination after refusing to sit in the back of a bus.

After his college sports career and military service, Robinson briefly played for the Kansas City Monarchs in the Negro Leagues, a baseball league for African American players.

This experience became the platform which led him to Major League Baseball, where he would later break the racial barrier by playing for the Brooklyn Dodgers in 1947.

His decision to play in the Major Leagues and his ability to deal with the intense racism and threats he endured with grace and determination became central to the struggle for civil rights and integration in American sports and society.

Jackie Robinson has had a storied career, and the moments of public enthusiasm and appreciation have been numerous.

- **Major League Baseball debut**. On April 15, 1947, when Jackie Robinson made his debut with the Brooklyn Dodgers, he became the first African American player to play in the Major Leagues in the 20th century. Although he faced hostility and prejudice, many in the audience greeted him with enthusiasm, understanding the historic importance of the moment.

- **The first home run**. On April 18, 1947, only days after his debut, Robinson hit his first major league home run against the New York Giants. It was a triumphant moment which signaled his ability and determination to succeed at the highest level of baseball.

- **Rookie of the Year winner**. At the end of his debut season in 1947, Robinson was honored as the Rookie of the Year, the best rookie of the year, recognizing his outstanding performance on the field.

- **The 1955 World Series**. Jackie played a key role for the Brooklyn Dodgers in their 1955 World Series victory, the first title in team history. His every move, especially in these crucial games, was the center of attention and he received public acclaim.

- **Last game and retirement**. When Robinson announced his retirement from baseball after the 1956 season, there was a great outpouring of affection and respect from fans and baseball fans. His last game and subsequent celebrations led many people to show their appreciation for all he had done for the sport and for American society.

- **The retirement of the number 42**. In 1997, MLB honored Jackie Robinson by retiring his number, 42, on all teams in the league. It was the first time in MLB history a number was retired for all teams. This act recognized his lasting impact on the game and demonstrated the deep respect and admiration baseball has for him.

Whenever Jackie Robinson took the field, he carried with him not only his extraordinary athletic abilities, but also the weight and hopes of an entire nation trying to overcome racial divisions.

The life lesson which Jackie Robinson still gives us today is based on breaking barriers. Robinson challenged and overcame racial barriers in professional baseball, proving talent and determination have no color. He embodied the fight for equality at a time when racism was deeply entrenched in American society.

He used his fame to raise awareness and fight against racial injustice, demonstrating one person can have a significant impact on society beyond his professional field.

He recognized the importance of solidarity, mutual support and unity, both on and off the field. He understood success in life, as in baseball, often depends on the ability to work together, support each other and aim for a common goal.

EQUALITY

Refers to the fair and impartial treatment of all people, regardless of differences such as gender, race, religion, sexual orientation, age, disability or any other distinguishing characteristic. It implies everyone has the same rights, opportunities, and access to resources, services, decisions, and benefits, without discrimination.

Equality goes beyond mere legality and is rooted in the moral and ethical fabric of a society. It is based on the principle every individual has inherent worth and is entitled to live without discrimination and to be treated with dignity and respect.

Equality is a pillar of social justice and an ideal toward which many societies aspire, recognizing that diversity is a strength and that when everyone is treated equally, the whole community benefits.

Chapter 11

MARIANO RIVERA
WHEN THE DREAM BECOMES LEGEND

Hi, little baseball fan!

Do you like to hear stories of champions who started from scratch and became heroes? Then you'll love the story of Mariano Rivera, baseball's spellbinder!

Imagine a little boy like you, only living far away in a small village called Puerto Caimito in Panama. Mariano didn't have shiny gloves or brand new bats.

He played baseball with gloves made of pieces of cardboard and sticks as bats.

Yet he had an incredible dream in his eyes and a burning passion in his heart.

When he wasn't playing baseball, Mariano was helping his father fish.

Can you imagine how many stories he had to tell after long days spent at sea, struggling against the waves and hoping for a good catch?

Yet the winds of fate were blowing hard for Mariano.

One day, people looking for new baseball talent noticed this boy with a powerful arm and incredible accuracy in throwing the ball.

And guess what?

Those scouts were from the New York Yankees, one of the most famous teams in baseball!

Mariano left his village and set off on an extraordinary adventure in New York. And as time went on, he became one of the brightest stars in baseball, never forgetting where he came from.

So whenever you dream big and it seems impossible, remember Mariano Rivera, the little boy from a small village who proved that with passion and dedication, dreams can come true.

And who knows?

Maybe one day you could be the one to tell your story like Mariano's!

Born on November 29, 1969, in Panama City, Panama, Mariano Rivera was not destined, at least initially, to be the greatest relief pitcher in baseball history.

Growing up in the small fishing village of Puerto Caimito, Mariano spent his childhood playing baseball with gloves made of cardboard and makeshift bats, far from the luxurious stadiums and spotlights of the Major Leagues.

His family was not wealthy, and like many other boys in his village, Mariano began working at a young age to help support his family. This lifestyle instilled in him a work ethic and determination he would later transfer into his baseball game.

Still fate had other plans for Rivera.

His extraordinary pitching ability soon put him in the spotlight.

In 1990, at just 20 years old, he signed his first professional contract with the New York Yankees, beginning a journey which would lead him to become one of the most iconic figures in modern baseball.

Despite his extraordinary success and international fame, Mariano never forgot his humble beginnings. He has always carried with him the discipline, humility and gratitude which characterized his youth in Panama.

These values, combined with his innate talent, have made him a great athlete as well as an inspiration to millions of people around the world.

Mariano Rivera, considered by many to be the greatest pitcher of saves in baseball history, had numerous moments when he electrified audiences and provoked enthusiastic reactions.

- **5 World Series saves**. In 1999, Mariano earned saves in all four games the Yankees won, as well as a fifth save in the ALCS. This display of stamina and skill sent the crowd into a frenzy and further cemented his legendary status

- **2003 ALCS Game 7**. Although the Yankees lost the series, Rivera pitched three perfect innings against the Red Sox, allowing his team to stay in the game and then win on an Aaron Boone home run. His dominance in the high-pressure environment was a demonstration of his invaluable value.

- **2004 All-Star Game**. Rivera was named MVP of the All-Star Game, an accolade that usually does not go to pitchers. His dominant performance in that game brought the entire stadium to its feet.

- **World Series**. Every time Mariano entered the game during the World Series, the atmosphere became electric. His presence on the mound was often synonymous with victory for the Yankees, and the fans knew it. During his many appearances in the final series, especially in the Yankees' victories in 1998, 1999, 2000, and 2009, Rivera was often the key to the team's success.

- **Record Saves**. In 2011, Mariano set the MLB record for the most career saves, surpassing Trevor Hoffman. When he got his 602nd save, the Yankee Stadium crowd went into a frenzy, paying tribute to his legendary pitcher.

- **After Injury**. In 2012, Rivera seriously injured his knee while taking batting practice. Many feared his career was over, yet Mariano returned in 2013 for one last triumphant season. His first appearance after the injury was emotionally charged, with the Yankee Stadium crowd on its feet the entire time.

- **Last Appearance at Yankee Stadium**. In 2013, in what would be his last game in Yankee Stadium, Rivera was sent out in the ninth inning. As soon as the notes of Metallica's *"Enter Sandman"* (his iconic entrance song) rang through the stadium, the crowd erupted in cheers and applause. His exit with Andy Pettitte and Derek Jeter coming to get him out of the game was an emotionally charged moment which left many fans in tears.

- **Ceremony to retire his jersey**. In 2013, the Yankees retired jersey number 42 in honor of Mariano Rivera. The entire stadium was on its feet, clapping and cheering, showing their love and respect for the great pitcher

- **Hall of Fame induction**. In 2019, Mariano Rivera became the first player in history to be elected to the Baseball Hall of Fame by a unanimous vote. The announcement and subsequent ceremony were emotional moments, with fans and players from around the baseball world showing their affection and respect for the great #42.

His talent, dedication and character made him an admired figure not only in New York, but throughout the baseball world.

IMPOSSIBLE BECOMES POSSIBLE

It is often used to say "a miracle has been accomplished" or *"an insurmountable obstacle has been overcome"*. These expressions emphasize surprise and admiration for an unexpected result or a goal achieved against all expectations. At other times, one might say *"all odds have been defied"* or *"what seemed unattainable has been achieved"*.

These phrases capture the essence of turning the unimaginable into reality.

Chapter 12

DEREK JETER
THE DIAMOND WIZARD

Have you ever had a dream of becoming a hero? Of being the person everyone is looking at at a decisive moment, hoping you will make magic? Well, close your eyes, because I am about to tell you the story of a boy who turned his dreams into reality in the glittering world of baseball.

Imagine a baseball field.

The sun is shining, the grass is bright green, and the stands are filled with fans eagerly awaiting the next play. Now, in the midst of it all, there is a little boy, with skinned knees and a great determination in his eyes. This child is Derek Jeter.

When Derek was little, he didn't have giant stadiums or bright lights around him. All he had was a worn glove, a wooden bat, and a dream the size of Yankee Stadium. He dreamed of playing for the most famous team in the world, the New York Yankees.

Every time he hit a ball, he didn't just see a field in his neighborhood, he imagined the cheering crowds and fireworks lighting up the night sky.

And you know what?

Derek didn't just dream.

He worked hard.

Day after day, practice after practice, he gave it his all. And every time someone told him he couldn't make it, he imagined sliding into home plate, under the bright lights of the stadium, with everyone cheering him on.

Want to know a secret?

Magic doesn't always come from a wand or a potion.

Sometimes, the real magic is the passion in a person's heart and the determination in his eyes.

Derek Jeter became a diamond magician, not because he had special powers, but because he believed in himself and followed his dream.

So the next time you dream of becoming a hero, remember Derek. And remember with a little imagination, passion and hard work, you too can create your own magic.

Open your eyes and think, "**What is your magic? What is your dream?**"

And like Derek, begin your journey to achieve it.

Born June 26th, 1974, in Pequannock, New Jersey, Derek Jeter grew up in a blended family. His father, Sanderson Charles Jeter, is African American and his mother, Dorothy, is of European descent. The diversity of his background enriched his education, giving him a unique perspective on the world and on sports.

Derek spent part of his childhood in Kalamazoo, Michigan. Here, his parents encouraged him and his sister Sharlee to pursue their dreams and work hard to achieve them. Even as a child, Jeter had a clear dream in mind: he wanted to play for the New York Yankees.

The baseball fields of Kalamazoo were his daily battlegrounds. He played whenever he could, honing his skills and imagining himself competing in the famous Yankee Stadium. Even during Michigan's cold winters, Jeter would not stop, practicing his moves and batting in the basement.

Derek's determination and work ethic led him to become a baseball star at Kalamazoo Central High School. These performances enabled him to be selected by the Yankees in the first round of the 1992 MLB draft.

Young Derek's dream was coming true.

From then on, Jeter never looked back, becoming one of the Yankees' most iconic figures, and also one of the greatest baseball players of all time.

Derek Jeter's origin story reminds you that no matter where you come from or what challenges you face, with determination, hard work and a little faith, dreams can come true.

Derek Jeter, throughout his illustrious career with the New York Yankees, has given countless unforgettable moments to his fans.

- **The Debut (1995).** When Derek Jeter made his debut with the Yankees, fans saw for the first time the future of their team. Although it was only the beginning, the excitement was palpable.

- **Rookie of the Year (1996).** In his first full year, Jeter won the American League Rookie of the Year title, proving he lived up to expectations.

- **World Series MVP (2000).** Jeter was named MVP of the 2000 World Series against the New York Mets, in which he demonstrated his ability in both defense and offense, leading the Yankees to victory.

- **"The Flip Play" (2001 ALDS)**. In a spectacular defensive move, Jeter made a backhanded throw to strike out a runner at home plate against the Oakland Athletics, keeping the Yankees ahead in the series.

- **Mr. November (2001 World Series)**. A few minutes after midnight, in the first World Series game played in November, Jeter hit a game-winning home run, earning him the epic nickname *"Mr. November"*.

- **The *"Dive Play"* (2004)**. During a game against the Boston Red Sox, Jeter made a spectacular dive into the stands to catch a foul ball, showing his dedication and lightheartedness for the game.

- **5th World Series (2009)**. Jeter's fifth World Series victory was a moment of great joy, both for him and Yankees fans. His leadership was instrumental in guiding the team to victory.

- **3,000th Hit (2011)**. Jeter reached the prestigious 3,000-hit club in spectacular style, hitting a home run in Yankee Stadium. The crowd went wild, and the standing ovation for Jeter was endless.

- **Moving into 6th place on the all-time hits list (2014)**. Passing Honus Wagner, Jeter moved up to 6th on MLB's all-time hits list, a feat in baseball history.

- **"*Derek Jeter Day*" ceremony (2014)**. Before his retirement, the Yankees celebrated "Derek Jeter Day" in his honor. The emotion-filled tribute saw fans and teammates pay tribute to the captain.

- **Last All-Star Game Appearance (2014)**. His last All-Star Game appearance was another emotional moment, with tributes from players and fans from across baseball.

- **Last MLB Game (2014).** Although it did not take place at Yankee Stadium, his last MLB game against the Boston Red Sox at Fenway Park was a special occasion, with opposing fans getting up to pay tribute to the legendary shortstop.

- **Last Appearance at Yankee Stadium (2014).** In one of the most emotional outings in baseball history, Jeter struck out a decisive run in his last home appearance at Yankee Stadium, giving the Yankees a win and a dream farewell to the fans.

- **Retirement of No. 2 jersey (2017).** The Yankees honored Jeter's legendary career by retiring his No. 2 jersey. During the ceremony, the crowd's ovation was deafening and echoed throughout the stadium.

His integrity, leadership and passion for the game have left an indelible mark on baseball history and the hearts of fans around the world.

FULFILLING DREAMS

Is about bringing to fruition the aspirations, ambitions and desires which reside deep in our hearts. It involves overcoming obstacles, facing challenges and persevering in the face of adversity to make concrete what was once only a thought or idea.

Realizing a dream often requires determination, passion, faith and commitment. It also implies the ability to listen to oneself, to believe in one's potential, and to have the courage to follow one's own path, even when deviating from traditional paths or when facing doubts and insecurities.

When a person succeeds in making concrete what he or she dreamed of, he or she not only achieves a personal goal, but often inspires others as well. It shows with dedication, commitment and a clear vision, it is possible to overcome any obstacle and turn deepest desires into reality.

It is important to remember that every dream is unique, as is the path to achieving it. There is no one-size-fits-all formula or defined time frame; what matters is the passion, energy and resilience with which you pursue and work to make it a reality.

Realizing dreams is a feature of the strength of the human spirit and its ability to create, innovate and transcend.

Chapter 13

YOGI BERRA
THE MAN WHO SPOKE WITH SMILES

Was there ever a time when you said something and everyone laughed, even though it wasn't exactly what you meant? Or maybe you asked a question and the answer confused you even more? Well, there was a man in the baseball world who was a master at this, and his name was Yogi Berra!

Imagine living in a big city called St. Louis and having a beautiful name like Lawrence. But one day, a friend of yours looks at you and says, *"Hey, you know? When you sit like that, you look like one of those wise meditation masters called yogis!"* And from that moment, everyone starts calling you *"Yogi"*. Funny, isn't it?

Yogi was not only famous for his strange nickname, but also for the funny things he said. Once, when asked what time it was, he said, *"It depends on where you are"*. And another time, talking about a popular restaurant, he said, *"No one goes there anymore, it's always too crowded"*. His jokes and witty phrases were so confusing that people couldn't help but laugh!

But Yogi was not only a comedian.

He wore a Yankees jersey and when he played, it was like seeing magic on the field.

So the next time you find yourself saying something funny remember Yogi Berra. And smile, because in the baseball world, he showed you can be both a great athlete and a person with infectious humor!

What do you say, would you like to have some "Yogisms" of your own?

Yogi Berra, whose real name was Lawrence Peter Berra, is one of the most iconic figures in American baseball and certainly one of the most beloved personalities in sports history. Born on May 12th, 1925, in St. Louis, Missouri, his origins are deeply rooted in an Italian immigrant family. The Berra family lived in a neighborhood called *"The Hill"* in St. Louis, an Italian-American community. Life was difficult for immigrants during that time; many were poor and tried to adapt to a new culture while keeping their own alive. Berra dropped out of school after the eighth grade and began working to help his family.

The nickname *"Yogi"* was given to him by a childhood friend who observed that Berra, sitting with his legs and arms crossed, resembled a yogi, or meditation master. This curious name would later make Berra even more recognizable in the decades to come.

Despite his humble beginnings, Berra showed an incredible talent for baseball. He began his youth career playing on local teams and in youth leagues, and it was not long before his talents were noticed by professional scouts. His professional career began with the New York Yankees, and Yogi became one of the most respected and accomplished catchers in MLB history.

In addition to his remarkable skills on the field, Berra is also famous for his *"Yogisms"* often humorous and contradictory phrases and sayings that reflected his unique and witty personality. One famous example is, *"It's not over until it's over"*.

Berra is a perfect example of how dedication, work ethic and a little humor can lead a person from humble beginnings to become a sports legend.

Yogi Berra, during his illustrious career with the New York Yankees, gave us numerous unforgettable moments.

- **Three-time MVP.** He won the American League's Most Valuable Player award three times (1951, 1954 and 1955), proving his ability and consistency year after year.

- **The *"Perfect Game"* of 1956.** During the 1956 World Series, pitcher Don Larsen threw a perfect game (a game without conceding bases to any opposing batter), with Berra as catcher. The moment when Berra jumped into Larsen's arms at the end of the game has become iconic in baseball history.

- **Double Heat Wave.** In the 1957 season, Berra surprised everyone with a double that led to the Yankees' victory in a decidedly tense game. The crowd went wild.

- **10 Championships Won.** Berra holds the record for most World Series won by a player. This is an unprecedented achievement that has given Yankees fans countless moments of joy.

- **Return as Manager.** After being fired by the Yankees in 1964, Berra returned as manager of the New York Mets in 1972, leading them to the World Series in 1973 with the slogan *"You Gotta Believe!"*

- **18 All-Star Games.** Berra was selected to participate in the All-Star Game as many as 18 times during his career, a testament to his consistent excellence on the field.

- **Retirement of his jersey**. In 1972, the New York Yankees retired jersey number 8 in honor of Yogi Berra, recognizing his impact and contributions to the team and the sport.

- **His *"Hall of Fame"* Induction**. In 1972, Yogi was inducted into the Baseball Hall of Fame. His acceptance and acceptance speech touched the hearts of many, recognizing his invaluable contributions to the sport.

- **Reconciliation with the Yankees**. After a period of alienation with Yankees management, Yogi Berra and the team finally buried the hatchet in 1999. His return to Yankee Stadium was an emotional moment for fans and for Berra himself.

- **Leadership Moments**. Although he was not known for being a great speaker, his ability to lead by example and handle complex personalities on teams often galvanized his teammates and inspired the audience.

- **Receiving the Presidential Medal of Freedom**. In 2015, just months before his passing, Berra was honored by President Barack Obama with the Presidential Medal of Freedom, the highest civilian award in the United States.

Yogi Berra's humor

Imagine you have a jigsaw puzzle with two pieces that look like they should go together, but when you try to put them together, they don't fit perfectly. Yogi Berra's humorous phrases are like those puzzle pieces. At first, what he says seems to make sense, but then you realize there is something strange or surprising about it.

It's as if he's saying, *"Imagine you're eating a chocolate cake ... but it's made of broccoli! The surprise and confusion makes it fun because you don't expect things to go that way"*. And then, you could share some of his phrases and laugh together as you try to figure out what he meant!

Below I list some of his most famous phrases.

"It's not over until it's over".
"It's like déjà vu all over again".
"Nobody goes there anymore because it's always too crowded".
"If you come to a fork in the road, take it".
"If you don't know where you're going, you might end up somewhere else".
"Baseball is ninety percent mental and the other half is physical".
"You can't think and hit the ball at the same time".
"The future is not what it used to be".
"If you can't imitate it, don't copy it".
"I said many things I never said".
"You can observe a lot just by looking".
"Always make a good first impression because you will never get a second chance to make a good first impression".

These *"Yogisms"* have become part of the American cultural fabric and are often quoted in both sports and non-sports contexts. The lighthearted and often profound nature of these phrases reflects Yogi Berra's unique and charming personality.

Yogi Berra's humor is largely based on cognitive dissonance.

Cognitive dissonance occurs when there are two conflicting thoughts or beliefs in a person's mind. Berra's sentences exploit this conflict by creating assertions which, on first reading, seem contradictory or make no sense.

This type of humor causes the reader or listener to pause briefly, a moment of confusion, followed by the realization of the paradox or ambiguity of the statement.

When Berra says something like *"It's not over until it's over"*, he leads us to reflect on the fact something may appear to be concluded before it actually is, but he does so in a way which sounds redundant and paradoxical. Also, many people tend to give up early in situations and stop pushing and struggling.

Or consider his phrase, *"No one goes there anymore because it's always too crowded"*.

The dichotomy between *"no one"* going to a place and the place being *"too crowded"* creates a cognitive dissonance which is both amusing and profound, as it highlights how certain places or events can become victims of their own success.

The phrase *"If you come to a fork in the road, take it"*, is confusing because the fork in the road is made up of two paths. You either take one or the other. However the concept of the phrase is much more subtle. It invites you to face the situation and choose which path to take.

In essence, don't stall, don't procrastinate, but take action.

His style of humor plays with words and ideas in surprisingly profound yet humorous ways.

Through this cognitive dissonance, Berra was able to make people think, make them laugh, and often share hidden wisdom behind his seemingly simple statements.

Each of these moments reaffirmed the legend of Yogi Berra being an outstanding baseball player, a cultural icon and a beloved American.

If you also learn this kind of humor, you will see that it will serve you well in life.

THE ART OF SMILE

Is more than just lip curving or a manifestation of happiness. It is a universal language, a powerful emotional expression that has the ability to connect human beings across cultural, language and geographic barriers. A smile can have a myriad of meanings. It can be a sign of welcome, understanding, comfort or pure joy. It can be a way to relieve tension, to show empathy or to celebrate a shared moment.

The art of the smile lies in its genuineness. An authentic smile can light up a face, reach the heart of the recipient and create an immediate bond. It has the power to soothe spirits, make ordinary moments special and create unforgettable memories. A smile is also an art in the deepest sense of the word.

Like any art form, it requires practice, presence and awareness. It requires the ability to be in tune with one's own emotions and those of others, to be vulnerable and open, and to share a piece of one's soul. In many cultures, a smile is considered a gift, a blessing that is offered freely and has the capacity to enrich the lives of the giver and the receiver. It is a silent but powerful demonstration of shared humanity, a bridge between souls and a reminder that, despite life's differences and challenges, there is a common language of love, joy and connection.

Ultimately, the art of smiling is an expression of the inherent beauty of the human spirit, a manifestation of the ability to find joy, hope and meaning in even the simplest moments of life.

Chapter 14

DARRYL STRAWBERRY
FROM STORM TO REBIRTH

Hey little champ, I bet you love stories about the great baseball players, right?

Those stories where the challenges seem insurmountable, the hero always finds a way to succeed. Let me tell you about a real hero, not the comic book kind, but a real one, on the baseball field. His name? Darryl Strawberry.

Now, imagine a player so formidable he could send the ball dancing through the sky like a shooting star every time he hit. Darryl was that kind of baseball wizard. However like all great heroes, he had his demons to fight.

And these demons were bigger and scarier than any opposing team.

Off the field, in his personal life, Darryl faced dark storms.

It was as if, after playing in bright sunshine, he returned home where storm clouds awaited him. But do you know what makes Darryl special? Even when these clouds seemed too dark and heavy, he never stopped looking for the light, and hope. And with the help of his faith, a magical power gave him strength and courage, he began to fight against these monsters, one day at a time.

You know when you're playing and you fall, and it seems impossible to get back up?

Then a friend comes along, or maybe your mom or dad, and they hold your hand, helping you get back on your feet.

Here, Darryl had a lot of help along the way, people who believed in him, who saw the hero in him, even when he had forgotten he was a hero.

Darryl Strawberry's story is not just one of home runs and victories in the field.

It is a story of falls and rises, of defeats and triumphs, of darkness and light.

As I tell you about his adventure, you will find every hero can find the strength to get back up, no matter how many times he falls.

Ready to discover this incredible journey?

I promise it will be an adventure you won't easily forget!

Darryl Strawberry is known not only for his outstanding talent on the baseball field, and also for his personal struggles off the diamond.

He has continually reinvented himself.

He has died many times only to be continually reborn.

Born March 12th, 1962, in Los Angeles, California. Growing up in Crenshaw, a neighborhood in Los Angeles, his childhood was not easy. He came from a disadvantaged family, and his father was known to be abusive. Darryl and his brothers often sought refuge from his father's abusive behavior by playing baseball outside the home. The sport, in a sense, became a saving grace for Darryl during his formative years.

Darryl's talent for baseball became evident as early as Crenshaw High School.

He was a powerful hitter, and his abilities on the field attracted the attention of professional baseball scouts. He was selected as the first overall pick by the New York Mets in the 1980 MLB draft.

His entry into professional baseball was meteoric.
Darryl won the National League Rookie of the Year award in 1983 and soon became one of MLB's most feared players. With the Mets, he won a World Series in 1986.

Darryl Strawberry, during his baseball career, gave many thrills to his fans.

- **Home Runs Clutch**. Darryl had an innate ability to hit home runs at critical times in games. When his team needed runs the most, he would often respond with a powerful hit off the field.

- **All-Star Games**. Strawberry was selected for the MLB All-Star Game eight consecutive times from 1984 to 1991. Each time he participated, fans expected great things from him, and he rarely disappointed them.

- **1986 World Series**. While playing for the New York Mets, Darryl played a key role in the team's victory in the 1986 World Series. His performances in those games were memorable and cemented his hero status among Mets fans.

- **Record of Home Runs with the Mets**. Darryl holds the record for home runs in a single season with the New York Mets, with 39 in 1987 and 1988. Every time he sent the ball over the fence, the crowd erupted in ovations.

- **1988 season**. During this season, Darryl put up some of his best career performances. He hit 39 home runs and had 101 RBIs, leading the Mets to the playoffs and thrilling the fans with his feats.

- **Comebacks**. Despite his personal problems, every time Darryl returned to the field after an absence, the public greeted him with great enthusiasm, hoping to see the stellar athlete they knew and loved.

- **1990 season**. Although the Mets did not have a great season, Darryl shined, reaching a career high in batting average, with .277, and leading the team in home runs and RBI.

- **Return to baseball after cancer**. Darryl was diagnosed with colon cancer in 1998. His battle and subsequent return to baseball were moments of pure inspiration. His first batting appearance after his diagnosis was an emotionally charged moment, with the audience on its feet applauding him.

- **His 300th home run**. In 1996, while playing for the New York Yankees, Darryl hit his 300th career home run. This milestone represented one of many peaks in his illustrious career, and fans celebrated this special moment with him.

- **His final season with the Yankees**. In 1999, despite battles with injuries and personal problems, Strawberry showed flashes of his old self, hitting important home runs in the playoffs and helping the Yankees win the World Series.

These episodes, in addition to many others, underscore Darryl's tumultuous but incredibly talented career.

During the 1980s and 1990s, Strawberry struggled with addictions to cocaine and alcohol.

These addictions had a direct impact on his career, leading him to miss many games and receive several suspensions from MLB.

In addition to his drug problems, Strawberry has had several legal problems.

He was arrested several times for drug possession, driving under the influence and, on one occasion, for assault with a deadly weapon. In addition, he was found guilty of tax evasion in 1995.

Because of his legal problems and probation violations, Strawberry spent time in prison. In 2002, he was sentenced to 18 months in prison for violating the terms of his probation.

Despite all these obstacles, he tried to get his life back on track after baseball.

He spoke openly about his addiction problems and tried to help others through his testimony. After overcoming his personal problems and addictions, Strawberry embraced the Christian faith and used his story as a testimony of the power of redemption and change through faith in Jesus Christ. With his wife Tracy, he founded "Strawberry Ministries" to help others find hope and transformation through the message of the gospel.

Darryl Strawberry's story serves as a powerful reminder about the dangers of addiction and the consequences it can have on a person's life. His ability to overcome these obstacles and seek greater meaning and purpose in his life after baseball also offers a message of rebirth and reinventing one's existence.

REINVENTING

Is a process of personal transformation through which an individual changes fundamental aspects of his or her life, personality, or ambitions in order to adapt to new circumstances or achieve higher goals. This path goes beyond simple change or adjustment; it is a complete and profound overhaul of the self, which can affect everything from career to personal relationships, from mental attitude to self-view. For you to accomplish this process, it is necessary to have a clear idea of what you want to become, a map that guides you through your transformation journey, and understanding who you are, what motivates you, and what your strengths and weaknesses are is the first key step. The last step after the vision, you need to develop a plan and act on it. This may include acquiring new skills, building new relationships, or adopting new behaviors and habits.

Reinventing oneself is an act of self-esteem and courage. It is a recognition that, despite previous circumstances or limitations, you have the power to take control of your life and shape it so that it is in harmony with your true essence and aspirations.

Chapter 15

KEN GRIFFEY JR.
THE BASEBALL SMILE

Hi, future champion!
Have you ever heard of a baseball star so bright and funny even adults called him *"The Kid"*?
His real name is Ken Griffey Jr.
His story makes you realize how magical baseball can be. Ken was born into a family where baseball was not just a game but a way of life.
Imagine growing up with a dad who is famous in the baseball world.
While most kids would wake up and watch cartoons, Ken would wake up and run outside to play baseball, dreaming of being like his father, Ken Griffey Sr. You can think of him as a superhero with a bat instead of a sword!
One of the most extraordinary things about Ken Jr. was his smile.
Every time he took the field, he had this bright, infectious smile, like he had just heard the funniest joke in the world.

And do you know why he smiled? Because he loved every single moment he spent playing. His passion was so evident you couldn't help but root for him.

But wait, there's more!

One of the most incredible things happened when Ken and his father played on the same team, the Seattle Mariners. Imagine for a moment: your father is on the field next to you.
And not only that!
In one magical game, they both hit home runs one after the other. It's as if Batman and Robin teamed up to beat the bad guys!

And do you know what Ken's story teaches us?
Baseball is not only a sport. It is, above all, a game, something you should love and enjoy. And if you have passion and determination, dreams can come true. So, the next time you're on the field, think of "*The Kid*" pull on your best smile, and enjoy every at-bat, pitch, and run. Who knows? Maybe someday they will tell your story like the new "*The Kid*"!

Ken Griffey Jr. was born in Donora, Pennsylvania, on November 21st, 1969.
His birth date is exciting because he shares the same day, albeit 49 years apart, with another baseball great, Stan Musial. It becomes even more fascinating when one considers both are initially from the same small town of Donora.
However Griffey's destiny in baseball was written long before he was born. His father, Ken Griffey Sr., was also a well-known baseball player, having played on several MLB teams, including the Cincinnati Reds, where he won two World Series. Ken Jr. grew up around baseball, spending a lot of time in the locker room and on the field with his father and seeing up close the exploits of the "*Big Red Machine*," the legendary Reds team of the 1970s.

Growing up in this environment fueled Junior's passion for baseball from a young age. He started playing as a boy and quickly became known for his incredible athletic ability and natural talent for the game. His youthful career led to his selection as the first overall pick in the 1987 MLB draft by the Seattle Mariners.

His roots in Donora, his connection to other baseball greats like Stan Musial, and his special bond with his father, a champion himself, provided Ken Griffey Jr. with a unique and rich context in baseball long before he began his remarkable professional career.

"The Kid" gave the public numerous unforgettable moments during his extraordinary baseball career.

- **Griffey at the Draft**. In 1987, the Seattle Mariners selected him as the first overall pick in the MLB draft. This event marked the beginning of his legendary career, and fans were thrilled to see a new emerging star.

- **First Home Run**. His first MLB home run came on April 30th, 1989, and it was clear early on that *"The Kid"* had an exceptional talent.

- **Father and Son**. One of the most exciting moments in baseball history occurred when Ken Griffey Jr. and his father, Ken Griffey Sr., hit home runs consecutively in a game in 1990. This unique event could unite generations of fans.

- **Chasing the home run record**. During the 1994 season, Griffey Jr. began with an extraordinary run-up for the home run record in a single season. Although he did not break the record, the anticipation and excitement among fans were palpable with each of his appearances.

- **Rescue in 1995**. During the division finals against the New York Yankees, Griffey scored the winning run by sliding home, sending the Mariners to the next round and saving baseball in Seattle.

- **10 consecutive Gold Gloves**. Between 1990 and 1999, Griffey Jr. won the Gold Glove for his outstanding defensive performance in the outfield for ten successive years, a recognition of his versatility as a player.

- **500th home run**. In 2004, Griffey Jr. hit his 500th home run in MLB, joining a very exclusive club and making fans elated about his remarkable career.

- **Return to Seattle**. In 2009, Griffey Jr. returned to the Mariners, the team with which he had started it all. The ovation he received upon his return home was extraordinary.

- **Last Outfield.** In 2010, Griffey hit the final home run of his career. Although he didn't know it then, fans were in a frenzy to see *"The Kid"* in action again.

- **All-Star Game MVP**. In 1992, Griffey Jr. won the MLB All-Star Game MVP (Most Valuable Player) award, showcasing his talent on one of the biggest stages.

- **Retirement of jersey No. 24**. In 2016, the Seattle Mariners retired Griffey's No. 24 jersey, honoring his incredible career with the team. The event was emotional and showed how much Griffey was loved by Seattle fans.

- **Hall of Fame induction**. In 2016, Griffey Jr. was inducted into the Baseball Hall of Fame with a record of 99.32 percent of the vote, the highest in history.

- **The incredible wall catch**. In addition to this, Griffey was known for his power at the plate and for his extraordinary defensive skills. One of his most famous catches occurred when he ran back to the outfield wall, jumped, and caught a ball about to become a home run, thus saving a run.

Griffey's ability to shine on both defense and offense, with his infectious smile and love of the game, made his every game a must-see for fans. He was, in many ways, the heart and soul of baseball during its peak years.

THE RELATIONSHIP BETWEEN DIFFERENT GENERATIONS

Represents a natural connective tissue in the fabric of society. Indeed, this interaction between different ages is not merely an exchange of words but a profound dialogue transcending time. Older generations, shaped by a world that has experienced deep transformations, bring stories, traditions, and life lessons. They lived in eras when technology was not yet predominant, where relationships and values had a different connotation than today. From them, younger people can learn resilience, the importance of patience, and the ability to appreciate the little things.

On the other hand, younger generations are growing up in a digitized, fast-paced, and ever-changing world. Through them, older generations can better understand current dynamics, gain a new worldview, learn to adapt to innovations, and embrace future challenges. These generational differences can sometimes generate misunderstandings or friction.

Often, the perception of an age gap leads to stereotypes or prejudices. Yet, when generations stop to listen to each other, they realize that despite the differences, there are many similarities in dreams, hopes, and fears. The beauty of the relationship between different generations lies in the balance between preservation and innovation. There is magic in seeing the past and the future dialogue in the present, enriching each other, and building a path that honors history and welcomes the new.

Chapter 16

SATCHEL PAIGE
DEFIANCE OF INJUSTICE

A legend was born in a small corner of America when the leaves danced to the rhythm of the wind and the stars shone like diamonds in the night sky.

This is not the story of a superhero in a mask or cape but of a boy named Satchel Paige who, armed with a ball and glove, was about to change the history of baseball and, in some ways, the world.

Imagine a young Satchel playing in the dirt streets of Mobile, Alabama. As his feet kicked up dust clouds, his mind wandered far away, dreaming of floodlit stadiums and frenzied crowds. But Satchel was no ordinary child, and his path would not be easy. As he was born in an era of deep racial divisions, many doors were closed to him.

Yet, his determination was indomitable.

With every pitch, Satchel challenged opposing batters and a system which wanted to relegate him to the margins. Even when he was told "*no*", when stadiums were divided, and dreams seemed far away, he believed in something more significant: justice. For Satchel, baseball was not just a game but a stage to prove everyone deserved equality and respect.

However challenges did not stop this ball hero.

With his inimitable technique, he began to earn everyone's respect and admiration.

He played on black teams, then across the continent, and finally against some of baseball's greatest icons. Every time he stepped onto the pitcher's mound, Satchel wasn't just pitching for a win, he was pitching for an ideal: the hope of a world where every child, regardless of the color of their skin, could play, dream, and become whoever they wanted to be.

Little Friend, Satchel Paige's story is a journey of passion and perseverance to achieve justice.

It is a lesson in how, with talent and tenacity, you can overcome any barrier.

And as I tell you about this extraordinary player, I hope you can see the accomplishments of a great athlete and the heart of a hero who fought for a better world. As Satchel said, "*Throw the ball and face life, and remember that the game is never over until you have played the last game*".

Leroy Robert Paige was born on a hot summer day in 1906 in Mobile, Alabama. It was difficult in America, where racial barriers were high and often impossible to cross. However, like many great people in history, Satchel was not one to break down in the face of obstacles.

His father, a manual worker, passed on to him a hard work ethic, while his mother, a tough and strong woman, instilled in him the importance of integrity and self-respect. These lessons would be crucial for Satchel in his formative years.

As a boy, difficulties were not lacking.

Paige spent time in a reform school after running into trouble with the law as a teenager. Luckily, he met a mentor who introduced him to structured baseball.

It was the beginning of a legend.

Satchel's determination and innate talent quickly got him noticed.

And as his talent grew, so did his reputation. Yet in a still profoundly segregated America, his talent only took him as far as the Negro Leagues. Still, he did not lose heart. In the Negro Leagues, Satchel not only became a superstar, he represented hope for all those young African Americans who dreamed of a better life through sports.

The nickname "*Satchel*" was given to him because of a temporary job as a porter at the train station, where he carried the luggage of travelers, or "*satchels*" in English. The name soon became synonymous with accuracy and mastery on the baseball field.

Paige was an outstanding baseball player and a symbol of determination, endurance, and breaking barriers. With every pitch, with every win, Satchel proved talent knows no color and barriers can be broken down with passion and dedication. His is the story of a baseball champion and of a man who, through sports, fought for justice and equality.

Satchel Paige was one of the greatest pitchers in baseball history.

- **His years in the Negro Leagues**. Before joining Major League Baseball, Paige played in the Negro Leagues, where he was an absolute superstar. During this time, he was known for outstanding performances and pitching shutouts against some of the best black teams of the era.

- **His MLB debut**. At 42, many thought Paige was too old for the MLB, but he proved otherwise. In 1948, he joined the Cleveland Indians. He helped the team win the World Series, becoming the oldest pitcher to debut in a World Series game.

- **His spectacular performances**. Paige was known for his charisma and ability to entertain the audience. Occasionally, he would call his outfielders to center field and strike out opposing batters individually.

- **Tribute in the MLB All-Star Game**. During his career, Paige was selected for several All-Star games in the Negro Leagues. Still, one of the most poignant moments was when he was honored before the MLB All-Star Game in 1953

- **Return to the major leagues at age 59. In 1965**, at age 59, Paige made a brief appearance with the Kansas City Athletics, becoming the oldest player to play a game in the MLB. Despite his age, he pitched three scoreless innings, again demonstrating his talent and resilience.

- **Challenging Legends**. He was known to issue open challenges to the best hitters of the era, inviting them to try to hit his pitches. These challenges became must-see events, and crowds would gather to see if the stars of the day could get the better of the great Satchel Paige.

- **His nicknames for the pitches**. Paige had particular names for his pitches, such as *"the whiz ball"* and *"the hesitant slow ball"*. These nicknames and his incredible skills added to the entertainment and drove the audience wild every time he stepped on the mound.

- **His election to the *"Hall of Fame"***. In 1971, Paige became the first Negro Leagues player elected to the *"Baseball Hall of Fame"*. This recognition not only honored his extraordinary career it was also a time of celebration for all those who had fought against racial injustice in baseball and elsewhere.

Whenever Satchel Paige took the field, one could be assured he would put on a show.

The story goes Paige often slept in his car or under the stands, traveling from town to town to pitch in any game he could. Although these stories were sometimes exaggerated, they contributed to Paige's myth and legend, making each of his appearances a must-see event.

He was also famous for a set of "***rules for staying young***" shared throughout his career. These rules were imbued with humor and wisdom, and they became famous over time.

Here are some of Paige's best-known "rules":
- Avoid fried foods, which anger the blood.
- If your belly collides with your chest, push your belly away.
- Hold your breath. This is the philosophy of the old Satchel: slow, deep breathing.
- Keep your love sincere.
- Run lightly until the old days catch up with you.
- Above all, don't look in the mirror. You might see yourself as you really are and fall down dead.
- Don't smoke.
- Avoid the use of alcohol.
- Don't look back at yourself.
- Go to bed at 10 o'clock at night.
- Don't worry about breaking the rules occasionally.

If you think back to when these rules were dictated, Paige had seen far. You will also do well to observe them as they are still fundamental today.

JUSTICE

Is one of the fundamental principles on which any community's social and moral order is based. It refers to fairness, impartiality, and uprightness, ensuring everyone receives what they are entitled to according to their rights and merits. Justice goes beyond mere enforcement of laws; it is imbued with ethics, fairness, and integrity.

In legal terms, justice represents the proper application of laws fairly and impartially, ensuring that no one is mistreated or discriminated against. It is the pillar on which the legal systems of democratic societies rest, committed to protecting the rights and freedoms of individuals. But justice also has a profoundly moral and philosophical dimension. It concerns questions of right, balance, and recognition of the inherent worth of every human being. It is an ideal to aspire toward, a goal to be achieved in social coexistence and interpersonal relationships. The importance of justice lies in its ability to create harmony and cohesion within a community. A just system generates trust, stability, and security among its members. In contrast, an unjust system can cause conflict, inequality, and tension. Unfortunately, justice is not always realized in practice. There are examples of injustice, discrimination, and abuse of power worldwide. However, the continuous aspiration for justice, the struggle for rights and equality, and the relentless pursuit of fairness represent hope and progress for humanity.

Chapter 17

HAMMERIN' HANK
FROM CHALLENGE TO LEGEND

Hey, big baseball fan!
Let me tell you an extraordinary story. It's one of those stories which gives you chills and makes your heart race. Once, a long time ago, a little boy named Henry was born in a small town called Mobile in Alabama.

As a little boy, he loved to play baseball using sticks and balls made of rags. But he knew deep in his heart one day, he would play on the big baseball fields in front of thousands of people.

That little boy became known as Hank Aaron, yet to the fans and those who looked up to him, he was *"Hammerin' Hank"* He was like a rocket launcher with a bat in his hand. When he hit the ball, it flew higher and farther than anything you had seen.

But the road for Hank was challenging.

He lived in a time when people were judged by the color of their skin, and many did not want him to achieve greatness. Still Hank was resilient. He faced challenges and obstacles with dignity and grace, showing the world his true fighting spirit.

Only some people were happy for him while he was on course to break the home run record. He received threatening letters and death messages, yet Hank never gave up.

He kept playing, giving his best, showing the world that with determination and courage, nothing is impossible.

Lace up your shoes, grab your bat, and, with the inspiration of "*Hammerin' Hank*", give your best!

Born February 5, 1934, in Mobile, Alabama, Aaron faced many challenges before becoming a baseball legend.

Hank Aaron grew up in an African-American family in the Deep South of the United States during the segregation period. Mobile was a port city which provided limited opportunities for a person of color. The Aaron family lived in poverty. Hank spent much of his youth in a scrapwood house without electricity or running water.

Aaron loved baseball from an early age.

His passion for the game led him to play at a semiprofessional level while still a teenager. After attracting attention with his skills, he joined teams in the Negro Leagues, playing briefly for the Mobile Black Bears and then the Indianapolis Clowns.

Aaron jumped to the Major Leagues in 1954 with the Milwaukee Braves (which later became the Atlanta Braves). His MLB career coincided with a tumultuous period in American history, particularly regarding civil rights. As he approached Babe Ruth's home run record, he received numerous death threats and hate messages. Still Aaron remained resolute and eventually set a new record of 755 career home runs, a milestone which stood for decades.

During his 23 seasons in the major leagues (1954-1976), he surpassed batting records set by some of baseball's greatest hitters, including Babe Ruth, Ty Cobb and Stan Musial.

Hank Aaron had many memorable moments in his career which captivated the public.

- **First Outfield**. On April 23rd, 1954, at only 20 years old, Hank Aaron hit his first career home run against the St. Louis Cardinals. This would be just the beginning of one of baseball's most impressive home run careers.

- **1957 World Series**. Aaron played a crucial role in the Braves' victory in the 1957 World Series against the New York Yankees. He had a .393 batting average during that series and hit three home runs.

- **3,000th Hit**. On May 17th, 1970, Aaron got his 3,000th career hit, a mark achieved by only a few in baseball history.

- **650th Home run**. On July 20th, 1973, Aaron hit his 700th home run, bringing him closer to Babe Ruth's record. This brought enormous attention and expectation for the next year when he would finally surpass Ruth.

- **715th Home run**. Without a doubt, the most iconic moment in Aaron's career was when he hit his 715th home run on April 8, 1974, breaking Babe Ruth's record (714). The moment was historic, and the crowd at Atlanta's Fulton County Stadium greeted him with a thunderous ovation.

- **755th and final Home run**. On July 20th, 1976, Aaron hit his 755th and final home run, setting a record that would remain unbeaten for decades, surpassed only by Barry Bonds with 762.

- **Retirement of Number 44**. When the Braves retired his Number 44 in his honor, the audience gave him a standing ovation, recognizing his immense contribution to the game and the team.

- **"Hall of Fame"**. During various ceremonies in which he was honored, such as being inducted into the *"Baseball Hall of Fame"* in 1982, the audience always greeted him with affection and admiration.

- **Return to Milwaukee**. Whenever Aaron returned to Milwaukee, where he began his career with the Braves before they moved to Atlanta, he received a warm welcome from fans who had watched him grow as a player.

- **Memorial ceremonies**. Even years after retirement, Hank Aaron was recognized or honored in various events; the audience showed affection and respect with loud applause.

- **All-Star Games**. Aaron was selected to the All-Star Game 25 times during his career, a record he shares with Willie Mays and Stan Musial. Each selection allowed fans to see him shine against baseball's best players.

- **Presidential Medal of Freedom (2002)**.

- **Miscellaneous records**. Aaron's batting records included 1,477 extra-base hits and 2,297 RBIs. 2,174 runs scored (second to Ty Cobb) and 12,364 times at bat (second to Pete Rose). His win total (3,771) was exceeded only by those of Cobb and Rose. Aaron's batting average was .305.

- **Gold Gloves**. He won 3 Gold Gloves (1958, 1959 and 1960).

- **Charitable events**. Hank Aaron was known for his philanthropic involvement and dedication to the community. At public events he attended, fans always greeted him with affection and admiration.

- **World Children Baseball Fair**. Deserving an absolute foreground is the story that saw Aaron Oh, two baseball champions, united for a grand project. When Aaron heard that there was a Japanese man, a certain Sadaharu Oh, who had hit more home runs than him (868), not only was our hero not upset or skeptical, but on the contrary, he was happy (despite racism, which between Americans and Japanese is even more insidious). He wanted to meet him by all means, and a great friendship was born. An international project to propagate baseball among young people around the world, the *"World Children Baseball Foundation"* took shape, and from it, the *"World Children Baseball Fair"* a prestigious annual camp, a kind of showcase for the best budding talent on the globe. Regarded as World Baseball Ambassadors, the *"odd couple"* formed by Aaron and Oh have been able to raise their sportsmanship to the skies, resetting barriers and divisions, racial and geographical, in a series of outreach initiatives.

Hank Hammerink, with his indomitable grit, enormous courage, and memorable deeds, etched his name in the pantheon of baseball. His legacy, forged by electrifying moments and unparalleled dedication, will remain an inspiring beacon for future generations of fans and players.

COURAGE

Is one of the fundamental human virtues, representing the ability to face and overcome fears, risks, and challenges, even in the presence of uncertainty or potential danger. It is not simply boldness or recklessness, it is rather a deep-seated determination which stems from conviction, passion, and, often, the need to do what one believes is right. The true essence of courage lies not in the absence of fear but in confronting it and deciding something is more important than fear itself. Courage is a light which guides through the darkness of uncertainty. This inner fire strengthens even in doubt and pushes through seemingly impossible limits. It is a fundamental pillar of human character, inspiring respect, admiration, and, often, hope.

Chapter 18

TOMMY JOHN
THE ART OF REBIRTH

I understand you are a baseball fan!
Want to hear a fantastic story which will make you realize how important it is to never give up? I will tell you about Tommy John, who turned a challenge into a victory in baseball and life.

Tommy was born to play baseball.

From an early age, everyone around him knew he was destined for great things every time he threw or hit the ball. As he grew up, his talent became unmistakable, and he entered the world of professional baseball. However like any great story, his had challenges to overcome.

One day, while on the mound, he felt a stabbing pain in his arm. It was as if his most precious tool, his pitching arm, had betrayed him. The doctors told him he had a severe injury and might never be able to play again.

Can you imagine how he felt?

It was as if his dream was shattered into a thousand pieces.

Yet Tommy had a lion's heart.

Instead of giving up, he underwent a risky new operation to repair his arm. Many people advised against it, still he was determined. He wanted to return to the field and prove to himself and the world with passion and determination, nothing is impossible.

And guess what?

After surgery and a lengthy rehabilitation, Tommy returned to play, and he did so with the strength and grit which few had ever seen. Not only did he become a great pitcher again, his story also symbolized hope and resilience.

The operation he had undergone even took his name, becoming a benchmark for other athletes facing similar injuries.

Here is the lesson we can learn from Tommy: in life, as in baseball, there may be times when everything seems to go wrong. However with courage, determination, and a little faith, we can overcome any obstacle and return stronger. Now, pick up your bat and hit your ball, dreaming big, just like Tommy John did!

Tommy John, whose full name is Thomas Edward John Jr., was born on May 22nd, 1943, in Terre Haute, Indiana. He grew up in a typical American environment, where baseball was more than just a pastime; it was a way of life, a symbol of American culture.

His family always supported him in his baseball aspirations. Growing up in Indiana, where the sport was deeply embedded in the social fabric, Tommy was determined to make his mark. With hard work, dedication, and the support of those around him, he succeeded, becoming one of baseball's most iconic figures, for his performance on the field and for his resilience in the face of adversity.

Tommy John is best known for his long and productive pitching career and, even more significantly, the revolutionary elbow surgery which bears his name, "Tommy John surgery."

Here are some of the highlights of his career in which the public particularly cheered him:

- **The Significant Victories**. Tommy John, throughout his 26-year career, has accumulated 288 victories. Each significant milestone, such as multiple wins of 20 games in a season, earned the public's admiration.

- **Return After Operation**. 1974, John suffered a severe elbow injury, leading to the revolutionary "Tommy John surgery." His ability to return to pitch at a high level after surgery in 1975 and earn a victory was a remarkable and widely celebrated feat.

- **World Series appearances**. Although he never won a World Series, John participated in several World Series with the Dodgers and Yankees. His performances in these high-stakes settings certainly earned the ovation of fans.

- **Final Years of Career**. Despite his advanced age for a sportsman, John continued to play well into his 46th year, receiving applause and accolades every time he took the mound, especially in the final seasons of his career, when the public knew that each game could be one of his last.

- **1979 season with the Yankees**. During this season, Tommy John had a record of 21 wins and only 9 losses, becoming one of the best pitchers in the league and earning a second-place vote for the American League's Cy Young Award.

- **Appreciation at the end of his career**. As he neared retirement, many stadiums across the United States paid tribute to Tommy John, recognizing his contributions to the game and his indomitable spirit in the face of adversity.

Each time Tommy John took the mound, he carried the story of a man who had overcome the odds to remain invalid for life. The audience always recognized him with enthusiasm and appreciation for his grit and determination.

The sun was beating down warmly on a small baseball field when a ball sank into the outfield turf. James, a ten-year-old boy passionate about baseball, had quickly run to catch it. But, in a moment of distraction, he had tripped, falling badly and twisting his ankle.

The pain was intense, and the fear even more so. Tears gushed from his eyes as he lay on the grass. *"What if I can never run again?"* he thought.

As his friends called for help and adults rushed in from all sides, a man slowly approached James. He was tall with a gentle, reassuring expression. James recognized him immediately; it was Tommy John, the legendary pitcher.

"Looks like you had a little setback," Tommy said, crouching beside the boy. *"But you know, I've been through tough times during my career, too"*. James nodded, trying to hold back tears, *"I'm afraid I can't play anymore, Mr. John"*. **Tommy smiled softly. "I understand your fear. But I will tell you one thing: when I had elbow surgery, everyone thought I would never throw a ball again. Instead, I came back stronger than before. And it wasn't just surgery; it was determination and passion for the game"**.

James looked wide-eyed at Tommy, listening to every word. **"The most important thing is not to give up, even when it seems impossible. Your leg will heal,** *and with the right help and determination, you will run faster than before*".

With those words, Tommy helped James sit down and wait for help. As the ambulance pulled away, James clutched his glove to his chest making a promise he would never betray. His heart was filled with courage, knowing that, like Tommy John, he too would overcome that obstacle.

REBIRTH

Is a profound and multifaceted concept which evokes the idea of a new beginning, regeneration, or resurrection. It represents a process by which an individual, community, or society regenerates, transforming, evolving, and finding meaning again after a period of decline, crisis, or symbolic death. In all its manifestations, rebirth involves transformation. It is a transition from an old self to a new one, from an old reality to a new one. It represents the eternal capacity of human beings and nature to regenerate, find new paths, and emerge renewed.

Chapter 19

TY COBB
BASEBALL'S INDOMITABLE FLAME

See the diamond over there? Imagine being in an old baseball stadium, the bleachers filled with fans in vintage hats and the screams of popcorn vendors in the air. In the crowd, there is one name which resonates more than the others: Ty Cobb.

He's who I'd like to introduce you to today, young baseball fan.

Ty Cobb was a true legend.

Born on December 18th, 1886, in an unincorporated community in Banks County, Georgia (GA).

He had a sparkle in his eyes from an early age that foretold great things. He had not had an easy start in life, thus difficulty hardened him, making him a fighter on the playing field.

When he played, Ty knew no half-measures.

Whenever he wielded the bat, he did so with fierce determination. It was not just about hitting the ball; it was about honor, about proving to himself and others what he was worth. His speed on the bases was astounding, and he was known for his ability to steal bases with cunning and daring.

Yet besides his prowess in the field, there was something even more special about Ty.

It was his resilience and his ability to overcome obstacles and criticism. At a time when baseball was very different from today, Ty Cobb broke record after record, setting standards that are still admired.

So whenever you feel something is too difficult or like giving up, think of Ty Cobb. Think about how, despite everything, he got up and gave it his all every single time.

Let his story remind you to trust yourself, to stand up for what you believe in, and to never let anything or anyone tell you that you can't do it. And who knows, one day you can become a legend like him.

Ty Cobb grew up in a profoundly Southern reality steeped in post-Civil War tensions. Cobb's early years were marked by challenges and tribulations. His childhood was marked by determination, a character trait which later influenced his baseball career. Cobb's passion for the game began at an early age, and soon, through his skill and commitment, he made his mark on local ballparks.

He signed his first professional contract at 18 with the Detroit Tigers. And while Cobb entered the major leagues with enormous expectations, he exceeded all expectations by becoming one of the greatest players ever.

Although he was known for his fiery temper and aggressive style of play, his determination and passion for the game were unmatched. He was a fighter, both on and off the field. With the right decision and ardor, one can overcome any obstacle.

Ty Cobb is considered one of the greatest baseball players of all time. During his career, he achieved multiple milestones.

- **Triple Crown Batting Champion**. In 1909, Cobb won the Triple Crown of hitters, leading the league in batting average, home runs, and RBI.

- **Batting Average**. Cobb has maintained a batting average above .400 in three seasons, a rare feat in baseball. His career batting average of .366 remains the highest in major league history.

- **Bases Per Batting (Total Bases)**. In 1909, Cobb led the Major Leagues with 296 bases per bat, an impressive figure that helped cement his reputation as one of the era's most Triple American League big hitters.

- **3,000 Hit Club**. In 1921, Cobb became the first player to reach 3,000 hits, a milestone very few players have achieved in baseball history.

- **American League Batting Champion**. He won the American League batting title 12 times, setting a record that still stands today.

- **Stolen Bases**. Although his total stolen bases figure was surpassed by later players, Cobb was a master at stealing bases during his era. He stole second base, third base, and home in the same game four times in his career, a record he shares with Honus Wagner.

- **Rivalry with Babe Ruth**. While Cobb represented the "dead-ball" era of baseball, Ruth represented the new era of home runs. Their on-field competitions created unforgettable moments for fans.

- **His final year with the Philadelphia Athletics**. Although most of his career was spent with the Tigers, Cobb spent his last two seasons with the

Athletics, proving he still had *"the stuff"* by batting .323 in the 1927 season.

- **Record runs scored**. At his retirement, Cobb held the record for the most runs scored in his career, a title he held for many decades.

- **RBI (Run Batted In)**. He led the American League in RBIs for four seasons, proving that he was a great runner and a formidable hitter in clutch situations.

- **Elected to the Hall of Fame**. In 1936, Cobb was selected as an inaugural member of the Baseball Hall of Fame, receiving 98.2% of the vote, the highest percentage among the players elected that year, including legends such as Babe Ruth and Honus Wagner.

- **Rivalry with Babe Ruth**. While Ruth changed the game with his home runs, Cobb represented the "old school" approach to baseball. This rivalry captured the public's attention both on and off the field.

- **Fists and fights**. While controversial, Cobb's frequent conflicts on the field made him a character to discuss and watch.

Ty Cobb's life was complex and often troubled, influenced by traumatic events and his combative personality.

He had a complicated relationship with his father, W.H. Cobb, an educator and a state senator. One of the most traumatic events in his life occurred when he was still a teenager: his mother shot and killed his father, apparently thinking he was an intruder.
Although she was cleared of murder charges, the incident deeply scarred Ty Cobb for life.

Off the baseball field, Cobb was an astute investor.

He made early investments in companies such as Coca-Cola and amassed considerable wealth. He was one of the richest baseball players at the time of his death.

TENACITY

Is the indomitable inner strength which drives an individual to persevere, persist, and not give up, even in the face of adversity, challenges, or seemingly insurmountable obstacles. More than mere determination, tenacity is a deep commitment to a goal or cause, an unwavering faith in one's mission or vision. It goes beyond sheer endurance; it is a burning passion, an inner flame which is not extinguished, regardless of external circumstances. It is the ability to see beyond immediate difficulties, to keep faith in the path taken, and to keep pushing forward, even when everything seems to be against you. Those who possess tenacity know success and achievement do not come quickly. They recognize behind every remarkable feat are defeats, mistakes, failures, and moments of doubt. However, what distinguishes tenacious people is their unwillingness to let these setbacks get them down. Instead of seeing obstacles as impossible, they see them as challenges. It is often fueled by a deeply personal motivation: a passion, a dream, a mission, or a sense of duty. It may stem from a desire to fulfill an ambition, help others, change the world, or overcome one's limitations. In many ways, tenacity is synonymous with resilience. Both represent the ability to face adversity and emerge from it strengthened, wise, and determined. Tenacity is a testament to the human spirit, our ability to strive, hope, and pursue our dreams, regardless of the odds or circumstances. It is a reminder anything is possible with commitment, passion, and a little persistence.

Chapter 20

WILLIE MAYS
INDOMINABILITY

O nce upon a time, a boy dreamed of flying in a faraway land called Alabama.
With an airplane?
With a rocket?
With wings?
No, no. No airplane, rocket, or wings, but with a baseball bat and a glove.
This boy's name was Willie Mays.

Imagine having a magic wand that allows you to do amazing things on the baseball field. Well, Willie didn't have a magic wand, but talent, and with a bat and a glove he could let his dreams take flight and reach for the stars.

Yet you know, it wasn't just his ability which made him special but his determination, infectious smile, and ability to show everyone dreams can come true with passion and hard work.

And just like Willie, you too can have the magic in you.

It's not just about playing baseball; it's about believing in yourself, respecting others, and pursuing your dreams, whatever they may be.

So, the next time you feel discouraged or think you are not good enough, remember the story of Willie Mays.

Let his passion, strength, and smile be your beacon, and maybe one day, you can fly high in the sky of your dreams. And who knows, you'll start to unleash some of that contagious magic on those around you.

Willie Mays, often nicknamed *"The Say Hey Kid"*, is among the most legendary baseball players ever. His story and origins are deeply rooted in the U.S. South, a region with a rich baseball heritage.

Born May 6th, 1931, in Westfield, Alabama, Willie grew up in a baseball-loving family. His father, Cat Mays, played baseball in a semiprofessional league and soon passed on his passion and skills to young Willie. While many African-American families in the South were engaged in the hardships of segregation and economic challenges, baseball became a refuge and a source of pride for the Mays.

Even as a boy, Mays displayed extraordinary talent. After attending Fairfield Industrial High School, he began his professional career playing for the Birmingham Black Barons. In 1951, at just 20 years old, he made his major league debut with the New York Giants beginning his legendary career.

Willie Mays, is considered one of the best baseball players ever. His career is studded with unforgettable moments and records.

- **MLB Debut**. Willie Mays made his major league debut with the New York Giants on May 25th, 1951. He hit his first home run a few days later, on May 28th.
- **The Catch**. During the first game of the 1954 World Series, Mays made one of the most famous catches in baseball history. He ran more than 150 feet to center field and caught a batted ball over his shoulder, with his back facing the plate. This play is known as *"The Catch"*.
- **National League MVP**. Willie Mays won the National League MVP award twice, in 1954 and 1965.
- **All-Star Games**. Mays was selected to the All-Star Game 24 times, a record he shares with Stan Musial and Hank Aaron.
- **4 Home runs in a Game**. On April 30th, 1961, Mays hit four home runs in a single game against the Milwaukee Braves, becoming the ninth player in MLB history to achieve this feat.
- **500th Home run**. Mays reached the 500 home run milestone on September 13th, 1965.
- **3,000 Hit Club**. On July 6th, 1970, Mays entered the exclusive 3,000-hit club.
- **Retirement**. Mays retired from professional baseball in 1973. He had accumulated 660 home runs at his retirement, the third-highest total in MLB history.
- **"Hall of Fame"**. Willie Mays was inducted into the *"Baseball Hall of Fame"* in 1979 in the first round of voting.
- **Jersey retirement**. The San Francisco Giants retired Mays' jersey number 24 in his honor.

His power, speed, defensive skills, and passion for the game left an indelible mark on baseball history.

An exceptional meeting

It was a clear, sunny day at the park. Jack, a 10-year-old boy with a burning passion for baseball, was trying to pitch and hit with his friends. But that day, despite his efforts, everything seemed to go wrong. Every pitch went wrong, and every at-bat failed to hit the ball.

Frustrated, Jack sat on the bleachers, his glove beside him, almost on the verge of giving up on his dream of becoming a great baseball player. It was at that moment that a familiar but unexpected figure approached him. It was none other than Willie Mays, *"The Say Hey Kid"* himself.

"Looks like you had a tough day, champ". Mays said reassuringly, sitting beside Jack.

Jack, wide-eyed with surprise and admiration, nodded. *"I can't do anything right today. I don't know if I'm cut out for baseball"*.

Mays laughed softly. ***"Look, we all have our bad days. Baseball, like life, is not just about hitting every pitch. It's about learning from your mistakes and never giving up"***.

Jack looked at the legendary player, absorbing every word.

"When I was young, like you, I had my setbacks. Yet every time I fell, I got up again. Every mistake I made taught me something new. And you know what? In the end, those mistakes made me the player I became".

Jack's eyes shone with hope. *"Really?"*

Mays nodded, ***"Absolutely. It is important to love what you do, put your best effort into it, and most importantly, have fun"***.

Then, Mays stood up, grabbed Jack's glove, and threw it gently into the air, catching it with an unmistakable grace. *"Come, let's do some throwing. I'll show you some tricks"*.

As the sun began to set, Jack and the baseball legend shared an unforgettable afternoon on the field, uniting generations through the magic and wisdom of the game.

And in this brief moment, under the shadow of *"Say Hey Kid"*, Jack not only found his passion for baseball renewed he also learned valuable lessons about life, resilience, and love of the game.

INDOMINABILITY

Indominability and indomitable are similar concepts and are often used interchangeably. However, we can discern subtle differences in how they are commonly understood. This term is less common than indomitability and focuses on the idea that one cannot be *"dominated"* or *"subdued"* suggesting resistance to external submission.

Indomitability, conversely, is a more common term which evokes the idea of something or someone which cannot be *"tamed"* or *"controlled"*.

Chapter 21

WALTER JOHNSON
THE SILENT SPEED OF THE GREAT TRAIN

At dawn, the baseball field was shrouded in a quiet serenity.

The light mist made everything ethereal and magical as if the field were suspended between dream and reality. Between these quiet moments, a young aspiring player with his shiny new glove was anxiously waiting for his practice to begin.

In the distance, a majestic figure was slowly advancing toward the field. It was Walter Johnson, "The Big Train," a living legend. Every step reminded him of stories and legends, games he had won, and pitches which had gotten fans talking a lot.

The child watched him, almost mesmerized by his presence.

Seeing the young man, Walter approached with a warm, friendly smile. ***"You have that light in your eyes he*** *said, the same light I had when I was your age and dreamed of playing in the big leagues".*

He then began to show him the magic behind each pitch, how the ball was to become an extension of his own body and soul. Patiently, he explained the position of the feet, the importance of balance, and the secret behind a powerful throw. But between technical lessons, Walter also shared stories of his life, of challenges and victories, of defeats which had made each success all the sweeter.

As the sun rose, the child, under Walter's guidance, threw his first ball with an accuracy and strength he did not know he had. In that moment, he understood baseball was not just a game but a metaphor for life. Thanks to Walter, he learned any dream can become a reality with passion, dedication, and the proper guidance.

Born on November 6th, 1887, in Humboldt, Kansas, Walter grew up in a rural environment.

Life in rural Kansas during the late 19th century was anything but easy. Physical labor and hard work were daily occurrences for farming families, which undoubtedly helped shape Johnson's physical strength and determination.

The Johnson family moved to Olinda, California, during Walter's teenage years. In California, Walter began to develop his baseball skills, playing in local leagues and demonstrating extraordinary talent as a pitcher.

His fame snowballed in the baseball community, and scouts soon noticed him. This led him to sign for the Washington Senators in 1907 and began his storied career in Major League Baseball.

In addition to his skills on the field, Walter Johnson was highly respected for his character. He was known to be a humble, kind individual of great integrity. This combination of talent and personality made him one of baseball's most beloved and respected figures.

Here are the top ten occasions when the public cheered Johnson:

- **The Strikeout Record**. In 1912, Johnson set an MLB record by throwing 16 strikeouts in a game.

- **56 Scoreless Innings**. In 1913, he set a record by throwing 56 consecutive scoreless innings, which remained unbeaten for many years.

- **American League MVP**. Johnson won the American League MVP award in 1913 and 1924, recognizing his outstanding performance during those seasons.

- **Win number 300**. In 1920, he reached 300 career wins, a goal coveted by every pitcher.

- **1924 World Series**. Johnson helped the Senators win the 1924 World Series, earning his only championship victory.

- **Win number 400**. 1927, he reached another impressive milestone, recording his 400th career victory.

- **Last Game Ovation**. In his final game in 1927, the audience gave him a standing ovation as a tribute to his outstanding career.

- **Retirement of his number**. Senators' number 28, worn by Johnson, was retired in his honor, recognizing his impact and contributions to the team.

- **Hall of Fame induction**. In 1936, Walter Johnson was among five inaugural players inducted into the Baseball Hall of Fame.

- **Posthumous tributes**. Even after his death, fans and the entire baseball community honored Johnson with various accolades, recognizing his place in baseball history.

On February 22nd, 1936, a special event happened on the banks of the Rappahannock River in Virginia. In his youth, George Washington threw a silver dollar across this river. However, this story is probably a myth since silver dollars were not minted.

However, the legend inspired the famous baseball pitcher Walter Johnson. Known as *"Big Train"* for the power of his pitching, Johnson had dominated baseball for 21 years, mainly with the Washington Senators. His powerful pitching had secured him a place in the National Baseball Hall of Fame.

After finishing his playing career, Johnson devoted himself to coaching. Still, he had never earned a championship trophy, partly because of powerful teams like the New York Yankees.

When Fredericksburg, George Washington's hometown, decided to celebrate the president's 204th birthday, they invited Johnson to attempt to replicate the mythical throw across the river. Although he was 48 years old, the challenge intrigued him. He prepared by throwing silver dollars on his farm and humorously informed the town his arm was getting stronger and stronger.

The chosen pitching location was 372 feet (113 meters), similar to the distance between the home plate and the baseball field wall. The challenge seemed difficult, with odds of 20-1 against him. In Johnson's favor was his powerful pitch traveled at over 90 mph, nearly 100 mph.

Many curious citizens had already attempted to throw objects across the river but without success. And despite the bitter cold and adverse conditions, an enthusiastic crowd gathered to witness the event, with even a live broadcast on CBS Radio.

Johnson dressed up and had three attempts. Although the first was unsuccessful, the second and third tosses miraculously reached the other side. The coin tossed at an impressive distance of 386 feet (118 meters), was recovered by an Italian named Pietro Yon.

The event was widely reported. Later, a congressman attempted to replicate Johnson's feat but failed, resulting in an unforgettable joke: *"This is not the first time a politician has thrown away our money."*

Walter Johnson's advice to a kid who is a little clumsy

"Hi, kid, said Walter with a warm smile, I see you're a little down. Do you want to talk baseball?" Charlie nodded, *"I don't know why I can't make a good pitch today."*

Walter sat beside him and said, **"Have you ever heard of rhythm? Every pitcher has a unique rhythm, like a song. And once you find your rhythm, pitching becomes like a dance"**.

Charlie looked at him, confused.

"You see, baseball is not just about strength. It's about rhythm, about feeling the ball and the glove as if they were a part of you. I would close my eyes in the mountains and hear the baseball song. And when I was pitching, it was like dancing to that song".

Charlie's face lit up, **"So I have to find my song?"**

Walter nodded, **"That's right. And remember, every pitcher has bad days. But what matters is how you respond to those days. Don't let a bad day stop you. Get up, find your song, and dance with it"**.

SPEED

When applied to our lives and our way of thinking and acting, takes on a meaning far beyond mere swiftness of movement. It symbolizes an ability to adapt and respond to challenges in a constantly changing world. Think about how essential it is in specific contexts to make timely decisions: an entrepreneur, for example, might be faced with a unique opportunity and need more time to weigh the pros and cons before acting. At such times, speed of thought becomes an essential virtue. It is not just a matter of speed it is also a demonstration of mental clarity, the ability to quickly assess complex situations and act consistently.

However, speed as a virtue does not imply rushing without reflection. On the contrary, it represents an optimal synthesis between thought and action, between assessing a situation and moving with determination. And in this balance lies its true essence: balancing the need to stop and reflect with the need to move forward and innovate, facing with courage and determination the challenges that life puts before us. In an age when everything moves frenetically, recognizing the value of speed, the ability to adapt and react with wisdom and readiness, is more essential than ever.

Chapter 22

CHRISTY MATHEWSON
BASEBALL'S HISTORIC TURNING POINT

In early spring 2015, after Derek Jeter retired, MLB.com launched a social media campaign to crown the new *"Face of Baseball"*.

The one who emerged strongly was the player widely considered the *"first face"* of baseball: Christy Mathewson.

Baseball in the early 20th century was considered an unrespectable game. Clandestine betting and acts of hooliganism often thickened within it. No mother took pleasure in her son playing baseball.

Most players had gone through traumatic experiences and had complicated families behind them. Very few had studied, and very rare were college students. We understand from the photos of the time their faces were always petrified, stern, and very hard. They were either from the coal mines or from the countryside. Looking at Mathewson's photos, one is struck by the smile, almost always the same: one which inspires confidence, is never arrogant, and welcomes, reassures, and makes you feel at home.

Christy Mathewson's virtue was to reverse this trend.

His combination of talent on the field and his charisma off the field made him a role model, and he became one of the first five members of the "*Hall of Fame*" in 1936.

The son of a farmer, Mathewson attended Bucknell University. He earned a three-year scholarship. He was a good student, a member of literary societies, and a rising star in football and baseball at that university.

Christy Mathewson, often nicknamed "Big Six," "*The Christian Gentleman*", or "*Matty*", was one of the greatest pitchers in baseball history. Born August 12th, 1880, in Factoryville, Pennsylvania, he became one of baseball's first superstars.

Christy Mathewson is fervently remembered for many notable moments and accomplishments during his illustrious career:

- **The 1905 World Series**. One of the most iconic moments of Mathewson's career was when he pitched three complete shutouts in six days during the 1905 World Series, leading the New York Giants to victory over the Philadelphia Athletics.

- **A Strikeouts Record**. Mathewson shared the record for strikeouts in a single game (so far) with 16, made on October 13th, 1905

- **Dueling with Mordecai "*Three Finger*" Brown**. Mathewson had a famous rivalry with Chicago Cubs pitcher Mordecai Brown. Their duels on the mound are legendary in baseball history.

- **37-win feat**. In 1908, Mathewson won an incredible 37 games, an accomplishment that solidified him even more as one of the greatest pitchers of the era.

- **Hall of Famer career**. With 373 career wins, Mathewson ranks first in the National League (tied with Grover Cleveland Alexander). His legacy was further cemented when he was elected to the *"Inaugural class"* of the Baseball Hall of Fame in 1936.

- **His Book**. Mathewson also wrote a book titled *"Pitching in a Pinch"*, which offered insights into baseball and his career. The book is valuable reading for baseball fans. It is a reminder of his impact as a player and ambassador for the game.

- **His Dominance over the Phillies**. During his career, Mathewson threw three no-hitters against the Philadelphia Phillies, demonstrating his dominance against that particular team.

- **His Role in Player Formation**. After his playing career, Mathewson had a brief stint as manager of the Cincinnati Reds. Although his managerial career was not long, he impacted many young players.

- **Baseball Educator**. In addition to his book, Mathewson helped create one of the first educational baseball films to educate and promote the game he loved.

All these moments, combined with his outstanding virtues and many other accomplishments on the field, cemented Christy Mathewson as one of the most admired and respected figures in baseball history.

During World War I, Mathewson served in the Chemical Warfare Service on the French front. During an exercise, he and other soldiers were accidentally hit by toxic gases due to a mistake. This exposure is believed to have contributed to the respiratory problems he would have later in life, eventually leading to his death. He died on October 7th, 1925, of tuberculosis.

Several anecdotes in his life help us frame the character.

Once, while pitching against a visibly clumsy rookie hitter, Mathewson stopped the game, stepped up to the plate, and advised the young man on how to hold the bat and position himself before returning to the mound and finishing the inning.

Friendship was of great value to him.

His deep friendship with McGraw, an impetuous and strong-willed player, evidenced this. He was considered a gentleman, apparently out of place. Instead, they shared an unwavering mutual respect and a steadfast, genuine friendship relationship when they played in the Giants.

Outside of baseball, Mathewson was an entrepreneur. He had interests in several businesses, including one in the bowling industry. He founded a bowling league and actively promoted the game.

He came out in 1912 with *"Pitching in a Pinch"*, a handbook on the game of baseball written uniquely by himself. The book offers an insight into the baseball world of the time, the merits and demerits of pitchers, and the characteristics of umpires. He mainly describes many human types humorously. He also wrote a play, *"The Girl and The Pennant"*, composed four-handedly with writer Rida Johnson Young (performed in 1913 and published in 1917), and a series of novels for children written beginning in 1911 in collaboration with W. W. Aulick (*"Won in the Ninth, First Base Faulkner"*, *"Second Base Sloan and Pitcher Pollock"*).

More than 110 years later, in the pages of his book, it is possible to trace valuable lessons even today. There is no doubt even today, we have much to learn from Mathewsonm, a true innovator and champion of versatility.

THE CAPACITY TO INNOVATE

in life transcends the mere introduction of new technologies or methods. It is about our ability to adapt, evolve, and grow in life's changing circumstances and challenges. It is the ability to look beyond the status quo, to see possibilities where others see barriers, and to have the courage to pursue visions even when they do not fit conventional paths. Innovating in life could mean readjusting one's habits and routines for better health, reinventing oneself professionally in response to changes in the job market, or revising one's beliefs and values in light of new experiences and knowledge. It can manifest itself in small everyday gestures or in significant life changes.

A key trait of personal innovation is **CURIOSITY**. The willingness to explore, learn, and understand is the basis of all progress. People who innovate ask questions, are unsatisfied with superficial answers and are willing to step outside their comfort zone.

Another crucial aspect is **RESILIENCE.** The road to innovation is rarely linear. There are obstacles, failures, and periods of doubt. The ability to persevere, to learn from mistakes, and to keep moving forward is what often distinguishes those who succeed in innovating from those who do not. Innovating in life requires a certain degree of open-mindedness. We live in a diverse and interconnected world, and the best solutions and ideas often emerge from the intersection of different disciplines, cultures, and perspectives.

CONCLUSION

During these pages, we have traveled across baseball fields, listened to the thunderous roar of crowds, and heard the heartbeats of legendary players. You relived the many exceptional moments which made baseball great.

But beyond the athletic feats and their outstanding hits, you really touched on the resonance of the human virtues that characterized these champions and remain the fundamental pillars of a life well lived.

For your convenience, I list the virtues covered in this book with the page where I talk about it next to it.

	PLAYER	*VIRTUE*	*Pg.*
1	Mike PIAZZA	**Humility**	*15*
2	Roberto CLEMENTE	**Compassion**	*25*
3	Babe RUTH	**Authenticity**	*31*
4	Jim ABBOTT	**Self-esteem**	*37*
5	Lou GEHRIG	**Gratitude**	*41*
6	Kirk GIBSON	**Determination**	*47*
7	Joe DIMAGGIO	**Being oneself**	*53*
8	Mo'ne DAVIS	**Fighting prejudices**	*59*
9	Jackie ROBINSON	**Equality**	*63*
10	Mariano RIVERA	**Impossible becomes possible**	*69*
11	Derek JETER	**From dream to reality**	*75*
12	Yogi BERR	**The art of smiling**	*81*
13	Darryl STRAWBERRY	**Reinventing**	*89*
14	Ken GRIFFEY JR.	**Relationship between generations**	*95*
15	Satchel PAIGE	**Justice**	*101*
16	Hammerin' HANK	**Courage**	*107*
17	Tommy JOHN	**Rebirth**	*113*
18	Ty COBB	**Tenacity**	*119*
19	Willie MAYS	**Indominability**	*125*
20	Walter JOHNSON	**Speed**	*131*
21	Christy MATHEWSON	**Innovation**	*137*

We ranged from the courage and determination of those who challenged prejudice to the authenticity and being themselves of those who showed the world their uniqueness without fear. We celebrated the innovation of players who revolutionized the game and the humility of those who, despite their extraordinary successes, remained deeply rooted and grateful. Each tile in this mosaic showed us that baseball, though a sport, reflects life's journey, a microcosm in which passion, tenacity, and equality are intertwined in an unforgettable dance.

And as we come to the end of this book, it is essential to remember that these stories and virtues do not just belong to the past. They are pillars for the present and for future generations.

They represent a testimony which, even in the modern world, there can be values and principles that remain unchanged, that are the basis of a whole and worthwhile life.

So, as we close these pages, be inspired by the lessons learned, not only to celebrate the game of baseball but to embrace and cultivate these virtues in our daily lives.

And always remember, as in a baseball game, every moment in life has the potential for something extraordinary.

BIBLIOGRAPHY

Angell Roger, *The Summer Game*, Viking Press, 1972

Appel M., Goldblatt B., *Baseball's best*, Mc Graw Hill, 1977

Asinof Eliot, *Eight Men Out*, Holt, 1963

Barzun Jacques, *God's Country and Mine*, Little, Brown and Company, 1954

Bouton Jim, *Ball Four*, World Publishing Co., 1970

Considine R., *The Babe Ruth story*, Pocket Books, 1948

Costas Bob, *Fair Ball: A Fan's Case for Baseball*, Broadway Books, 2000

Cramer Richard Ben, *Joe DiMaggio: The Hero's Life*, Simon & Schuster, 2000

Creamer Robert, *Babe: The Legend Comes to Life*, Simon & Schuster, 1974

Dickey G., *The history of American league baseball*, Scarborough Book Stein and Day Publishers, 1980

Dorfman H.A., *The Mental Game of Baseball*, Diamond Communications, 1989

Ealo J., *Béisbol, Cuba*, Editorial Pueblo, 1984

Golenbock Peter, *Dynasty: The New York Yankees*, 1949–1964, Prentice-Hall, 1975

Gonzalez R., *The pride of Havana*, Oxford University Press, 1999

Halberstam David, *Summer of '49*, William Morrow and Co., 1989

Kahn Roger, *A Flame of Pure Fire*, Harcourt Brace, 1999

Kahn Roger, *The Boys of Summer*, Harper & Row, 1972

Kinsella W.P., *Shoeless Joe*, Houghton Mifflin, 1982

Kurlansky Mark, *The Eastern Stars*, Riverhead Books, 2010

Leavy Jane, *Sandy Koufax: A Lefty's Legacy*, HarperCollins, 2002

Lee A., *The National League story*, Hill and Wang, 1961

Parrott H., *The lords of baseball*, Praeger Publishers, 1976

Posnanski Joe, *The Soul of Baseball*, William Morrow, 2007

R. Kahn, *A season in the sun*, Harper & Row, 1977

Reichler J., *The game and the glory*, Englewood Cliffs, Prentice-Hall, 1976

Ritter Lawrence, *The Glory of Their Times*, William Morrow, 1966

Schwartz Larry, *For Love of the Game*, Algonquin Books, 1992

Seymour H., *Baseball: the golden age*, Oxford University Press, 1971

Smith R., *Baseball*, Simon and Schuster, 1970

Turbow Jason, *The Baseball Codes*, Pantheon, 2010

Turkin H., Thompson S.C., *The official encyclopedia of baseball*, A.S. Barnes & Co., 1979

Will George, *Men at Work: The Craft of Baseball*, HarperCollins, 1990

Thank you for purchasing and reading this book

If you found it useful please visit the site where you bought it and write a review, even a short one. Your feedback is very important to me and will help other readers in their decision to buy my book.

https://www.amazon.com/review/create-review?asin= B0CLNH378L

Thank you very much!

John Jay Lewis

Made in the USA
Columbia, SC
08 February 2024

31593124R00083